touchPOINTS™
for men

TYNDALE HOUSE PUBLISHERS, INC.
CAROL STREAM, ILLINOIS

Visit Tyndale online at www.tyndale.com.

TYNDALE, Tyndale's quill logo, *New Living Translation*, *NLT*, and the New Living Translation logo are registered trademarks of Tyndale House Publishers, Inc.

TouchPoints is a trademark of Tyndale House Publishers, Inc.

TouchPoints for Men

Previously published under ISBN 978-1-4143-2018-2 and 978-0-8423-3307-8

General editors: Ronald A. Beers, V. Gilbert Beers, Amy Mason

Contributing writers: V. Gilbert Beers, Rebecca Beers, Brian R. Coffey, Jonathan Farrar, Jonathan Gray, Sean A. Harrison, Sandy Hull, Amy E. Mason, Rhonda K. O'Brien, Douglas J. Rumford, Linda Taylor

Designed by Jennifer Ghionzoli

ISBN 978-1-4143-7828-2

Printed in the United States of America

18   17   16   15   14   13   12
7   6   5   4   3   2   1

INTRODUCTION

PSALM 119:91, 160 | *Your regulations remain true to this day, for everything serves your plans. . . . The very essence of your words is truth; all your just regulations will stand forever.*

PSALM 119:105 | *Your word is a lamp to guide my feet and a light for my path.*

PSALM 119:111, 162 | *Your laws are my treasure; they are my heart's delight. . . . I rejoice in your word like one who discovers a great treasure.*

What a treasure we have in the living Word of God! The Holy Bible is relevant to today's issues and gives solid guidance for daily living. In *TouchPoints for Men* you will find more than one hundred topics, in alphabetical order; each topic is followed by questions, Scriptures, and commentary that tells you what the Bible says about it. The table of contents contains a complete listing of the topics for quick reference. While we could not cover every topic, question, and Scripture related to the subject of this book—men— our prayer is that you will continue to deliberately search God's Word to grow closer to God and discover how following his manual for living brings great joy and satisfaction. Whether you read through this book page by page or use it as a reference for topics of particular interest to you, may you find your answers in God's Word as you make it your daily guide.

Enjoy your treasure hunt!

The editors

2 TIMOTHY 3:16 | *All Scripture is inspired by God and is useful to teach us what is true and to make us realize what is wrong in our lives. It corrects us when we are wrong and teaches us to do what is right.*

CONTENTS

ACCOUNTABILITY

Why is accountability so important?

PROVERBS 12:15 | *Fools think their own way is right, but the wise listen to others.*

Good advisers can keep you from doing things that might hurt you or others.

What happens when there is no accountability?

JUDGES 17:6 | *In those days Israel had no king; all the people did whatever seemed right in their own eyes.*

1 SAMUEL 13:11-13 | *Saul replied, ". . . You didn't arrive when you said you would. . . . So I felt compelled to offer the burnt offering myself before you came." "How foolish!" Samuel exclaimed. "You have not kept the command the LORD your God gave you. Had you kept it, the LORD would have established your kingdom over Israel forever."*

Without accountability, people always tend to sin. The consequences eventually hurt you, hurt others, and pull you away from God.

How do I become more accountable?

JEREMIAH 23:24 | *"Can anyone hide from me in a secret place? Am I not everywhere in all the heavens and earth?" says the LORD.*

If you're going to take accountability seriously, you have to begin with God. You will better understand what you are doing and why you are doing it when you understand for whom you are doing it. God knows all the secrets of your heart anyway, so why try to hide anything from him? Be honest with God, and tell him the struggles you have in following him.

PROVERBS 27:6 | *Wounds from a sincere friend are better than many kisses from an enemy.*

Purposefully choose wise friends who will hold you accountable. Their honesty may hurt at times, but it can save you from greater pain down the road.

How can I effectively hold someone else accountable?

TITUS 1:7-8 | *He must not be arrogant or quick-tempered. . . . He must live wisely and be just. He must live a devout and disciplined life.*

In order to help others with accountability, you must hold yourself accountable first. Not only should you know God's commands, but you should consistently try to obey them and work to develop good judgment. If you are going to minister to others by holding them accountable, you must be wise, honest, godly, trustworthy, and kind yourself.

Promise from God 1 JOHN 2:3 | *We can be sure that we know him if we obey his commandments.*

ADULTERY

What is God's definition of adultery?

HEBREWS 13:4 | *Give honor to marriage, and remain faithful to one another in marriage. God will surely judge people who are immoral and those who commit adultery.*

Adultery is being unfaithful to your spouse. In general, this involves having a sexual relationship with someone other than your wife. But even unfaithful thoughts or an intimate emotional relationship with another woman can become adulterous if it takes you away from your wife.

MARK 10:11 | *Whoever divorces his wife and marries someone else commits adultery against her.*

The commitment to remain faithful till "death do us part" is serious. It should not be taken lightly.

MATTHEW 5:28 | *Anyone who even looks at a woman with lust has already committed adultery with her in his heart.*

When you look lustfully at another woman, you are being unfaithful to your spouse.

Why is adultery dangerous?

EXODUS 20:14 | *You must not commit adultery.*

God has commanded you to be faithful to your wife— committing adultery is blatant disobedience.

PROVERBS 6:27-29 | *Can a man scoop a flame into his lap and not have his clothes catch on fire? Can he walk on hot coals and not blister his feet? So it is with the man who sleeps with another man's wife. He who embraces her will not go unpunished.*

Like most sin, adultery is an act of momentary pleasure that can have dire and lasting consequences—a lifetime of regret and pain.

1 CORINTHIANS 6:9-10 | *Don't you realize that those who do wrong will not inherit the Kingdom of God? . . . Those who indulge in sexual sin, . . . or commit adultery, . . . none of these will inherit the Kingdom of God.*

Even if you are not caught in your sin during your lifetime, you won't get away with it forever.

How can I protect myself from adulterous relationships?

PROVERBS 2:16 | *Wisdom will save you from the immoral woman, from the seductive words of the promiscuous woman.*

JAMES 1:5 | *If you need wisdom, ask our generous God, and he will give it to you.*

Wisdom gives you the discernment you need to avoid adultery. You still must make the choice to avoid it, but having God's wisdom will help you recognize early warning signs that you are moving in the wrong direction.

PROVERBS 4:25-27 | *Look straight ahead, and fix your eyes on what lies before you. Mark out a straight path for your feet; stay on the safe path. Don't get sidetracked; keep your feet from following evil.*

If looking lustfully at women other than your spouse might lead you into adultery, then not looking at them that way will help you avoid adultery. It can be challenging, but having "faithful eyes" is one of the keys to successfully avoiding adultery.

PROVERBS 5:3-4, 7-9 | *The lips of an immoral woman are as sweet as honey, and her mouth is smoother than oil. But in the end she is as bitter as poison, as dangerous as a double-edged sword. . . . So now, my sons, listen to me. Never stray from what I am about to say: Stay away from her! Don't go near the door of her house! If you do, you will lose your honor and will lose to merciless people all you have achieved.*

When faced with adulterous temptations, don't be tempted to think that you can handle it. The best course of action is to run away and not look back.

PROVERBS 5:15, 18 | *Drink water from your own well—share your love only with your wife. . . . Let your wife be a fountain of blessing for you. Rejoice in the wife of your youth.*

You are more likely to commit adultery when you allow discontentment to creep into your heart. You won't be tempted to "shop around" if you are content with your wife and rejoice in the blessing she is to you.

Promise from God MATTHEW 5:8 | *God blesses those whose hearts are pure, for they will see God.*

ANGER

Why do I get angry?

NUMBERS 22:29 | *"You have made me look like a fool!" Balaam shouted.*

Anger is often a reaction to hurt pride.

GENESIS 4:4-5 | *The LORD accepted Abel and his gift, but he did not accept Cain and his gift. This made Cain very angry, and he looked dejected.*

1 KINGS 22:18, 27 | *"Didn't I tell you?" the king of Israel exclaimed to Jehoshaphat. "He never prophesies anything but trouble for me. . . . 'Put this man in prison, and feed him nothing but bread and water until I return safely from the battle!'"*

ESTHER 3:2, 5 | *Mordecai refused to bow down or show [Haman] respect. . . . When Haman saw that Mordecai would not bow down or show him respect, he was filled with rage.*

When people are confronted, rejected, ignored, or don't get their own way, anger is a common reaction.

1 SAMUEL 18:8 | *"What's this?" [Saul] said. "They credit David with ten thousands and me with only thousands."*

Anger is often a reaction to feelings of jealousy over what others have or what they have accomplished.

When is anger appropriate?

JOHN 2:15-16 | *[Jesus] drove out the sheep and cattle, scattered the money changers' coins over the floor, and turned over their tables. Then, going over to the people who sold doves, he told them, "Get these things out of here. Stop turning my Father's house into a marketplace!"*

Anger over sin is not only appropriate but necessary.

When I am angry, what should I avoid?

JAMES 3:5 | *The tongue is a small thing that makes grand speeches. But a tiny spark can set a great forest on fire.*

Avoid speaking your mind when you are angry. More often than not, you will regret words and actions that result from your overreacting to a situation.

1 SAMUEL 19:9-10 | *As David played his harp, Saul hurled his spear at David. But David dodged out of the way, and leaving the spear stuck in the wall, he fled and escaped into the night.*

Avoid acting on impulse in the heat of anger. You may do something that will haunt you for the rest of your life.

Everybody gets angry at times. What should I do when I get angry?

EPHESIANS 4:26-27 | *"Don't sin by letting anger control you." Don't let the sun go down while you are still angry, for anger gives a foothold to the devil.*

Stay under the control of the Holy Spirit through prayer, and try to resolve your anger quickly.

Promise from God PSALM 103:8-9 | *The LORD is compassionate and merciful, slow to get angry and filled with unfailing love. He will not . . . remain angry forever.*

ATTITUDE

What kind of attitude does God want me to have?

1 CORINTHIANS 13:4-7 | *Love is patient and kind. Love is not jealous or boastful or proud or rude. It does not demand its own way. It is not irritable, and it keeps no record of being wronged. It does not rejoice about injustice but rejoices whenever the*

truth wins out. Love never gives up, never loses faith, is always hopeful, and endures through every circumstance.

An attitude of love.

PHILIPPIANS 2:5, 7-8 | *You must have the same attitude that Christ Jesus had. . . . He gave up his divine privileges; he took the humble position of a slave and was born as a human being. When he appeared in human form, he humbled himself in obedience to God and died a criminal's death on a cross.*

An attitude of humble servanthood.

PHILIPPIANS 4:4 | *Always be full of joy in the Lord. I say it again—rejoice!*

An attitude of joy for all God has done for you.

PHILIPPIANS 4:6 | *Don't worry about anything; instead, pray about everything. Tell God what you need, and thank him for all he has done.*

An attitude of dependence on him for all your needs.

What kind of attitude is displeasing to God?

GENESIS 4:6-7 | *"Why are you so angry?" the LORD asked Cain. "Why do you look so dejected? You will be accepted if you do what is right. But if you refuse to do what is right, then watch out! Sin is crouching at the door, eager to control you. But you must subdue it and be its master."*

An attitude of anger and resentment.

NUMBERS 21:5 | *"Why have you brought us out of Egypt to die here in the wilderness?" they complained. "There is nothing to eat here and nothing to drink. And we hate this horrible manna!"*

An attitude of complaining and ungratefulness.

PROVERBS 18:12 | *Haughtiness goes before destruction.*

An attitude of pride.

What is the key to having a good attitude?

ROMANS 8:6 | *Letting your sinful nature control your mind leads to death. But letting the Spirit control your mind leads to life and peace.*

ROMANS 12:2 | *Don't copy the behavior and customs of this world, but let God transform you into a new person by changing the way you think.*

Let God's Holy Spirit, rather than your sinful nature, control your mind.

Promises from God MATTHEW 5:5, 8 | *God blesses those who are humble, for they will inherit the whole earth. . . . God blesses those whose hearts are pure, for they will see God.*

AUTHORITY

Why is human authority necessary?

JUDGES 21:25 | *In those days Israel had no king; all the people did whatever seemed right in their own eyes.*

1 PETER 2:13-14 | *For the Lord's sake, respect all human authority—whether the king as head of state, or the officials he has appointed. For the king has sent them to punish those who do wrong and to honor those who do right.*

God has instituted human authority to bring order and security to society. Authority in the business world, the church, and the family has the same purpose. Properly exercised, it is essential in teaching others, caring for others, and holding others accountable.

What if I have a bad attitude toward authority?

HEBREWS 3:7-10 | *The Holy Spirit says, "Today when you hear his voice, don't harden your hearts as Israel did when they rebelled, when they tested me in the wilderness. There your ancestors tested and tried my patience, even though they saw my miracles for forty years. So I was angry with them, and I said, 'Their hearts always turn away from me. They refuse to do what I tell them.'"*

Sometimes you might get tired of being told what to do: You want to chart your own course and become your own person. But being your own person and rebelling against authority are two very different things. Authority is not a bad thing—the abuse of authority is a bad thing. God's authority—his rules—not only will save your life but will lead you to success and blessing. Don't rebel against his authority, because you will jeopardize your very soul. Being your own person doesn't mean doing whatever you want; it means using your God-given personality and talents to serve him by serving others.

Is seeking to gain a position of authority a bad thing?

MATTHEW 20:26 | *Whoever wants to be a leader among you must be your servant.*

JOHN 3:30 | *He must become greater and greater, and I must become less and less.*

Don't seek positions of authority for the sake of power or self-promotion or blind ambition. If you want to be looked up to by others, then have a servant's heart, be willing to take responsibility for your actions (not passing the buck when it's convenient), refuse to stay silent when things are wrong, and do not seek glory for yourself. The world has taught you to look and act cool, to disrespect authority, and to bend the rules as far as you can. But in the end, it's the people who have consistently lived with kindness, integrity, and a deep love for God who will be most respected and honored.

Promise from God PROVERBS 29:2 | *When the godly are in authority, the people rejoice.*

BIBLE

How can a book written so long ago be relevant for me today?

ISAIAH 40:8 | *The grass withers and the flowers fade, but the word of our God stands forever.*

2 TIMOTHY 3:16-17 | *All Scripture is inspired by God and is useful to teach us what is true and to make us realize what is wrong in our lives. It corrects us when we are wrong and teaches us to do what is right. God uses it to prepare and equip his people to do every good work.*

HEBREWS 4:12 | *The word of God is alive and powerful. It is sharper than the sharpest two-edged sword, cutting between soul and spirit, between joint and marrow. It exposes our innermost thoughts and desires.*

Because the Bible is the Word of God, it is the only document that is "living"—in other words, it is relevant for all people in all places in all time periods. It is as contemporary as the heart of God and as relevant as your most urgent need.

What is promised to me when I read and study the Bible?

JEREMIAH 15:16 | *When I discovered your words, I devoured them. They are my joy and my heart's delight, for I bear your name, O LORD God of Heaven's Armies.*

The Bible sustains and directs you mentally, emotionally, and spiritually, bringing lasting joy and deep satisfaction in life.

JOHN 8:32 | *You will know the truth, and the truth will set you free.*

Reading the Bible tells you how to be set free from sin.

PSALM 119:9 | *How can a young person stay pure? By obeying your word.*

Reading the Bible helps you know how to stay pure.

PSALM 119:50 | *Your promise revives me; it comforts me in all my troubles.*

Reading the Bible refreshes you and gives you hope for the future.

PSALM 119:52 | *I meditate on your age-old regulations; O LORD, they comfort me.*

Reading the Bible gives you comfort in the face of fears and hurts in your life.

Can the Bible give me guidance?

PSALM 119:24 | *Your laws please me; they give me wise advice.*

PSALM 119:105 | *Your word is a lamp to guide my feet and a light for my path.*

Reading the Bible guides you in daily living, giving you the best counsel for your problems. It helps you discover and live out God's purpose for your life. The Word of God is from the mind and heart of God—who can deny that the all-wise, all-powerful, ever-present God is the best guide of all?

Promise from God PSALM 119:89 | *Your eternal word, O LORD, stands firm in heaven.*

BLAME

Is it possible to live a blameless life?

1 CORINTHIANS 1:8 | *He will keep you strong to the end so that you will be free from all blame on the day when our Lord Jesus Christ returns.*

COLOSSIANS 1:22 | *He has reconciled you to himself through the death of Christ in his physical body. As a result, he has brought you into his own presence, and you are holy and blameless as you stand before him without a single fault.*

There is no way that you, by your own efforts, can ever live a blameless life. It is only through Christ's dying on the cross that you become blameless in God's eyes. Christ took on the blame that you deserve. When you give Jesus control of your life and confess your sins to him, his forgiveness cleanses you. This doesn't mean that you no longer sin but that God looks at you as though you have not sinned.

Since it is impossible for me to live blamelessly, does it really matter if I sin sometimes?

PHILIPPIANS 2:14-15 | *Do everything without complaining and arguing, so that no one can criticize you. Live clean, innocent lives as children of God, shining like bright lights in a world full of crooked and perverse people.*

Your responsibility is to live as an example of Christ. To do this, you must do your best to keep your heart and mind pure. Imperfection is no excuse for sinning willfully.

Promise from God 2 CORINTHIANS 13:11 | *Be joyful. Grow to maturity. Encourage each other. Live in harmony and peace. Then the God of love and peace will be with you.*

BROKENNESS

What is meant by brokenness? How can it be important in my life?

PSALM 51:17 | *The sacrifice you desire is a broken spirit. You will not reject a broken and repentant heart, O God.*

Brokenness signifies the breaking of your pride and self-sufficiency. It means being aware of your full dependence on God. Brokenness often comes through circumstances that overwhelm you or through sin that seduces you. Those who are open about their brokenness—just as Moses, David, Jesus, and Paul were—can have great influence in the healing of others.

JOB 2:8-9 | *Job scraped his skin with a piece of broken pottery as he sat among the ashes. His wife said to him, "Are you still trying to maintain your integrity? Curse God and die."*

The alternative to brokenness is bitterness, which leads to dissatisfaction and general irritation with life. Bitterness prevents you from allowing God to heal you, for a bitter person looks inward instead of upward.

JOB 42:5-6 | *I had only heard about you before, but now I have seen you with my own eyes. I take back everything I said, and I sit in dust and ashes to show my repentance.*

Brokenness comes when you understand the contrast between God's holiness and your own sinfulness, and this realization humbles your heart. God promises to draw close to you when you are brokenhearted about sin in your life. When you turn to God in brokenness over your sin, he begins to heal and restore you.

ISAIAH 66:2 | *I will bless those who have humble and contrite hearts, who tremble at my word.*

One result of brokenness is humility. You come to the realization that you cannot fix all your problems, nor can you control all your needs. Acknowledging your dependence on God allows him to help you with your needs.

Promise from God 1 PETER 5:10 | *He will restore, support, and strengthen you, and he will place you on a firm foundation.*

BURNOUT

How do I know if I am experiencing burnout?

PSALM 69:1-2 | *Save me, O God, for the floodwaters are up to my neck. Deeper and deeper I sink into the mire; I can't find a foothold.*

You may be experiencing burnout if your life feels overwhelming and everyday tasks seem impossible.

JEREMIAH 45:3 | *I am overwhelmed with trouble! Haven't I had enough pain already? And now the LORD has added more!*

If you become exhausted and are in despair during a long stretch of work, if it seems as if your work will never be done, or if you are in a rut and can't seem to get out, you may be experiencing burnout. When you are burned out, you may even become bitter toward God.

What are some antidotes for burnout?

EXODUS 18:21-23 | *Select from all the people some capable, honest men. . . . They will help you carry the load, making the task easier for you. If you follow this advice, . . . then you will be able to endure the pressures.*

Delegate some of your workload. This can ease your burden, multiply your effectiveness, and give other people the opportunity to grow.

1 KINGS 19:5-8 | *As [Elijah] was sleeping, an angel touched him and told him, "Get up and eat!" . . . So he ate and drank and lay down again. Then the angel of the LORD came again and touched him and said, "Get up and eat some more, or the journey ahead will be too much for you." So he got up and ate and drank, and the food gave him enough strength to travel forty days and forty nights to Mount Sinai, the mountain of God.*

Take good care of your body by exercising, resting, and eating nutritious meals. Poor nutrition and unhealthy habits invite burnout.

ISAIAH 30:15 | *Only in returning to me and resting in me will you be saved. In quietness and confidence is your strength.*

MATTHEW 11:28-29 | *Jesus said, "Come to me, all of you who are weary and carry heavy burdens, and I will give you rest. . . . And you will find rest for your souls."*

When you are burned out, turning to the Lord for help is the key to renewal and refreshment. The strength you need to persevere through life's work and difficulties comes only from God. He promises to carry your burdens for you, giving you the rest you need.

Promise from God ISAIAH 40:29-31 | *He gives power to the weak and strength to the powerless. Even youths will become weak and tired, and young men will fall in exhaustion. But those who trust in the LORD will find new strength. They will* *soar high on wings like eagles. They will run and not grow weary. They will walk and not faint.*

BUSINESS

What principles should guide the way I conduct my business?

ECCLESIASTES 9:10 | *Whatever you do, do well.*

EPHESIANS 6:6-7 | *As slaves of Christ, do the will of God with all your heart. Work with enthusiasm, as though you were working for the Lord rather than for people.*

The way you work reveals the nature of your commitment to Christ. Hard work done with excellence and integrity honors God and builds a reputation that will stick with you your whole life and into eternity. Success in business may also bring material resources that you can use for God's glory.

DEUTERONOMY 25:15-16 | *Always use honest weights and measures, so that you may enjoy a long life in the land the LORD your God is giving you. All who cheat with dishonest weights and measures are detestable to the LORD your God.*

EZEKIEL 22:12 | *There are hired . . . loan racketeers, and extortioners everywhere. They never even think of me and my commands, says the Sovereign LORD.*

You should be honest. God condemns cheaters who use dishonest means to become successful. Always conduct your business aboveboard and in public, with no hidden kickbacks or shady deals.

PSALM 112:5 | *Good comes to those who lend money generously and conduct their business fairly.*

It is important to be generous in your business dealings. God promises that it is an investment that will pay off later!

AMOS 8:4-5 | *Listen to this, you who rob the poor and trample down the needy! You can't wait for the Sabbath day to be over and the religious festivals to end so you can get back to cheating the helpless.*

If you serve God in your business during the week, you live in harmony with what you profess on Sundays. If you exploit your workers during the week, it negates any faith you claim on Sunday.

LUKE 14:28 | *Don't begin until you count the cost.*

Whenever you start a project or business venture, plan ahead and make sure you can handle the costs—not only financially, but physically, relationally, and spiritually as well.

JAMES 4:13-15 | *Look here, you who say, "Today or tomorrow we are going to a certain town and will stay there a year. We will do business there and make a profit." How do you know what your life will be like tomorrow? Your life is like the morning fog—it's here a little while, then it's gone. What you ought to say is, "If the Lord wants us to, we will live and do this or that."*

Whatever business ventures you pursue, remember that God is in control and that you are completely dependent on him in everything.

Promise from God PSALM 37:37 | *Look at those who are honest and good, for a wonderful future awaits those who love peace.*

CALL OF GOD

Has God called me to do specific things?

ECCLESIASTES 11:9 | *Do everything you want to do; take it all in. But remember that you must give an account to God for everything you do.*

God gives you the freedom to follow many different roads and pursue many different activities over the course of your life—but remember that you will have to answer to him for everything you do. Not everything you do is a call from God, but everything you do is accountable to God.

1 CORINTHIANS 12:4, 7 | *There are different kinds of spiritual gifts, but the same Spirit is the source of them all. . . . A spiritual gift is given to each of us so we can help each other.*

2 TIMOTHY 4:5 | *Work at telling others the Good News, and fully carry out the ministry God has given you.*

God gives each individual a spiritual gift (sometimes more than one!) and a special ministry in the church. You can use your gifts to help and encourage others and to bring glory to his name. When you use these specific spiritual gifts, you help fulfill the purpose for which God made you.

How do I know what my calling is?

PSALM 119:105 | *Your word is a lamp to guide my feet and a light for my path.*

The first step to knowing your calling is getting to know God better by reading his Word. As God communicates to you through the Bible, he will show you what he wants you to do and where he wants you to go.

DANIEL 1:17 | *God gave [Daniel, Shadrach, Meshach, and Abednego] an unusual aptitude for understanding every aspect of literature and wisdom.*

God has given every individual special aptitudes and abilities. They provide the biggest clues to what God wants from you. As you develop those special abilities and begin to use them, you will see how to use your God-given gifts to get the job done.

ROMANS 12:2 | *Don't copy the behavior and customs of this world, but let God transform you into a new person by changing the way you think. Then you will learn to know God's will for you, which is good and pleasing and perfect.*

When you let God transform you by the power of his Holy Spirit, he will literally begin to change the way you think so that you will know what he wants you to do.

Promise from God 1 THESSALONIANS 5:23-24 | *May the God of peace make you holy in every way. . . . God will make this happen, for he who calls you is faithful.*

CHARACTER

What are the attributes of godly character?

EZEKIEL 18:5-9 | *Suppose a certain man is righteous and does what is just and right. He does not feast in the mountains before Israel's idols or worship them. He does not commit adultery. . . . He is a merciful creditor, not keeping the items given as security by poor debtors. He does not rob the poor but instead gives food to the hungry and provides clothes for the needy. He grants loans without interest, stays away from injustice, is honest and fair when judging others, and faithfully obeys my decrees and regulations. Anyone who does these things is just and will surely live, says the Sovereign LORD.*

Justice, righteousness, mercy, honesty, fairness, faithfulness, and generosity are essential traits of godly character.

How can I develop these godly character traits?

DEUTERONOMY 8:2 | *Remember how the LORD your God led you through the wilderness for these forty years, humbling you and testing you to prove your character, and to find out whether or not you would obey his commands.*

You are not born with godly character; it is developed through getting to know God and his Word and through experience and testing..

Promise from God ROMANS 5:4 | *Endurance develops strength of character, and character strengthens our confident hope of salvation.*

CHEATING

What does God think of cheating? Is it always wrong?

PROVERBS 11:1 | *The LORD detests the use of dishonest scales, but he delights in accurate weights.*

Cheating violates God's holiness. Cheating and godliness are not compatible.

Are some kinds of cheating worse than others?

MARK 12:40 | *They shamelessly cheat widows out of their property and then pretend to be pious by making long prayers in public. Because of this, they will be more severely punished.*

Sin is sin, but some sin receives greater punishment from God. Cheating those who are less fortunate and then trying to appear pious to others is a double sin—first, the sin of cheating, and second, the sin of hypocrisy. God has very strong words of warning for hypocrites.

How do I cheat myself?

LUKE 16:10 | *If you are faithful in little things, you will be faithful in large ones. But if you are dishonest in little things, you won't be honest with greater responsibilities.*

When you cheat, you are actually cheating yourself out of the best that God planned for you.

How do I cheat God?

MALACHI 3:8 | *Should people cheat God? Yet you have cheated me! But you ask, "What do you mean? When did we ever cheat you?" You have cheated me of the tithes and offerings due to me.*

You cheat God when you do not give to him what he deserves of your time, your money, your service, or your heart.

Promise from God PSALM 32:2 | *What joy for those whose record the LORD has cleared of guilt, whose lives are lived in complete honesty!*

CHRISTLIKENESS

━━━━━━━━━━━━━━━━━━━━━━━━━━━━•●

What is Christlikeness?

LUKE 9:23 | *[Jesus] said to the crowd, "If any of you wants to be my follower, you must turn from your selfish ways, take up your cross daily, and follow me."*

Christ gives us the ultimate example of how to live a life that is pleasing to God. To be like Christ, then, is your goal—if you pattern your life after him, you will please God. You will begin to think his thoughts, show his attitudes, and live as he would live here on earth today.

LUKE 6:36 | *You must be compassionate, just as your Father is compassionate.*

A compassionate lifestyle is a sign of Christlikeness.

JOHN 13:14-15 | *Since I, your Lord and Teacher, have washed your feet, you ought to wash each other's feet. I have given you an example to follow. Do as I have done to you.*

1 PETER 2:21, 23 | *God called you to do good, even if it means suffering, just as Christ suffered for you. He is your example, and you must follow in his steps. . . . He did not retaliate when he was insulted, nor threaten revenge when he suffered. He left his case in the hands of God, who always judges fairly.*

A life of humble service is a part of Christlikeness.

How can I show Christlikeness to others?

LUKE 6:32-33 | *If you love only those who love you, why should you get credit for that? Even sinners love those who love them!*

And if you do good only to those who do good to you, why should you get credit? Even sinners do that much!

You are like Christ to your enemies when you treat them with Christ's love.

MATTHEW 5:44 | *I say, love your enemies! Pray for those who persecute you!*

GALATIANS 5:22-23 | *The Holy Spirit produces this kind of fruit in our lives: love, joy, peace, patience, kindness, goodness, faithfulness, gentleness, and self-control. There is no law against these things!*

When Christ lives in and through you, you show Christlikeness to others. You can't do it on your own—Christ does it in you and through you.

Promise from God GALATIANS 2:20 | *My old self has been crucified with Christ. It is no longer I who live, but Christ lives in me. So I live in this earthly body by trusting in the Son of God, who loved me and gave himself for me.*

CHURCH

Why should I be involved in church?

PSALM 27:4 | *The one thing I ask of the LORD—the thing I seek most—is to live in the house of the LORD all the days of my life, delighting in the LORD's perfections and meditating in his Temple.*

PSALM 84:4 | *What joy for those who can live in your house, always singing your praises.*

Even though God lives in the heart of every believer, he also lives in the community of the church. When the church gathers together, it meets God in a special way. Just as going to a concert or sports event is so much more exciting than watching it on TV, participating with other believers in worshiping God is much more meaningful.

HEBREWS 10:25 | *Let us not neglect our meeting together, as some people do, but encourage one another, especially now that the day of his return is drawing near.*

Good friends are a wonderful gift, but fellowship with other believers at church is unique because the living God is in your midst. The church brings together people who have a common perspective on life. Christian fellowship provides a place for honest sharing about the things that really matter, for encouragement to stay strong in the face of temptation and persecution, and for unique wisdom to deal with problems.

What kinds of things should the church do?

MATTHEW 28:18-20 | *Jesus came and told his disciples, "I have been given all authority in heaven and on earth. Therefore, go and make disciples of all the nations, baptizing them in the name of the Father and the Son and the Holy Spirit. Teach these new disciples to obey all the commands I have given you."*

One of the primary jobs of the church is to bring the Good News of salvation to those who haven't heard it, to help them become believers, to baptize them, and to teach them God's truth.

ACTS 2:42, 44 | *All the believers devoted themselves to the apostles' teaching, and to fellowship, and to sharing in meals (including the Lord's Supper), and to prayer. . . . And all the believers met together in one place and shared everything they had.*

Key functions of the church include teaching, fellowship, worship, and prayer.

ACTS 13:2-3 | *The Holy Spirit said, "Dedicate Barnabas and Saul for the special work to which I have called them." So after more fasting and prayer, the men laid their hands on them and sent them on their way.*

It is the church's responsibility to send out missionaries, who will make God's truth known to those who have never heard the Good News.

1 TIMOTHY 5:3 | *Take care of any widow who has no one else to care for her.*

JAMES 5:14-15 | *Are any of you sick? You should call for the elders of the church to come and pray over you, anointing you with oil in the name of the Lord. Such a prayer offered in faith will heal the sick, and the Lord will make you well. And if you have committed any sins, you will be forgiven.*

The church should pray for members who are facing adversity and should take special care of widows, orphans, and those in need.

2 TIMOTHY 4:2 | *Preach the word of God. Be prepared, whether the time is favorable or not. Patiently correct, rebuke, and encourage your people with good teaching.*

The church has the special role of teaching and preaching God's Word.

Promise from God MATTHEW 16:18 | *Upon this rock I will build my church, and all the powers of hell will not conquer it.*

COMMITMENT

Why is commitment important?

PSALM 25:10 | *The LORD leads with unfailing love and faithfulness all who keep his covenant and obey his demands.*

When you are committed to following God, he will lead you to discover his will for your life, the satisfying and fulfilling purpose for which he created you.

PSALM 31:23 | *The LORD protects those who are loyal to him.*

When you are committed to God, he is committed to watching out for you and caring for you.

RUTH 1:16 | *Wherever you go, I will go; wherever you live, I will live. Your people will be my people, and your God will be my God.*

Commitment is a mark of true friendship.

1 CORINTHIANS 13:7 | *Love never gives up, never loses faith, is always hopeful, and endures through every circumstance.*

Commitment to others is evidence of love for them.

What should be my most important commitments?

MATTHEW 22:37-38 | *Jesus replied, "'You must love the LORD your God with all your heart, all your soul, and all your mind.' This is the first and greatest commandment."*

To love and honor God in all you do.

GENESIS 2:24 | *A man leaves his father and mother and is joined to his wife, and the two are united into one.*

HEBREWS 13:4 | *Give honor to marriage, and remain faithful to one another in marriage. God will surely judge people who are immoral and those who commit adultery.*

To love and be devoted to your wife.

PROVERBS 22:6 | *Direct your children onto the right path, and when they are older, they will not leave it.*

To love your children and teach them to love God.

JOHN 13:34-35 | *I am giving you a new commandment: Love each other. Just as I have loved you, you should love each other. Your love for one another will prove to the world that you are my disciples.*

To love others as God has loved you.

Promise from God **HEBREWS 3:14** | *If we are faithful to the end, trusting God just as firmly as when we first believed, we will share in all that belongs to Christ.*

COMPASSION

How does God show his compassion to me?

PSALM 72:12-14 | *He will rescue the poor when they cry to him; he will help the oppressed, who have no one to defend them. He feels pity for the weak and the needy, . . . for their lives are precious to him.*

PSALM 103:8 | *The LORD is compassionate and merciful, slow to get angry and filled with unfailing love.*

LAMENTATIONS 3:22-23 | *The faithful love of the LORD never ends! His mercies never cease. Great is his faithfulness; his mercies begin afresh each morning.*

God shows his compassion to you by not giving you the punishment you deserve. Instead, he gives you blessings you don't deserve, forgiving you and transforming you into what you were intended to be.

How can God's compassion to me help me be more compassionate to others?

1 JOHN 3:17 | *If someone has enough money to live well and sees a brother or sister in need but shows no compassion—how can God's love be in that person?*

God has the ultimate compassionate heart and demonstrates this love to his children freely. One mark of a godly man is the ability to share the compassionate heart of Jesus with others.

Promise from God PSALM 145:9 | *The LORD is good to everyone. He showers compassion on all his creation.*

COMPETITION

Is competition good?

1 CORINTHIANS 9:24 | *Don't you realize that in a race everyone runs, but only one person gets the prize? So run to win!*

Competition can motivate you to improve yourself and sharpen your skills.

When does competition become a bad thing?

2 TIMOTHY 2:5 | *Athletes cannot win the prize unless they follow the rules.*

Competition is unhealthy when it causes you to sin. If winning becomes everything, you may be tempted to compromise your integrity.

LUKE 18:11 | *The Pharisee stood by himself and prayed this prayer: "I thank you, God, that I am not a sinner like everyone else. For I don't cheat, I don't sin, and I don't commit adultery. I'm certainly not like that tax collector!"*

Competition can lead you to compare yourself to others. This can lead to pride, and pride leads to trouble.

MATTHEW 18:1-4 | *The disciples came to Jesus and asked, "Who is greatest in the Kingdom of Heaven?" Jesus called a little child to him and put the child among them. Then he said, . . . "Unless you turn from your sins and become like little children, you will never get into the Kingdom of Heaven. So anyone who becomes as humble as this little child is the greatest in the Kingdom of Heaven."*

Competition is inappropriate in matters of faith and in the eyes of God any time it causes you elevate yourself above others.

People say I can be too competitive at times. How can I learn to lighten up?

PHILIPPIANS 2:3-4 | *Don't be selfish; don't try to impress others. Be humble, thinking of others as better than yourselves. Don't look out only for your own interests, but take an interest in others, too.*

There's nothing wrong with a competitive nature as long as you are not competing for wrong things or out of wrong motives. Control your competitive nature before it causes you to hurt someone else.

COLOSSIANS 3:23 | *Work willingly at whatever you do, as though you were working for the Lord rather than for people.*

You should always do your best, rather than besting others. Doing your best honors the God who created you. If besting others is your only goal, you are selfishly trying to honor yourself.

Promise from God 1 CORINTHIANS 15:57 | *Thank God! He gives us victory over sin and death through our Lord Jesus Christ.*

COMPLAINING

What is it about complaining that is so wrong?

DEUTERONOMY 6:16 | *You must not test the LORD your God as you did when you complained at Massah.*

JAMES 5:9 | *Don't grumble about each other, brothers and sisters, or you will be judged.*

Complaining is often a form of criticizing God, his Word, and others, and it tests everyone's patience. Complaining focuses on what you don't have rather than on what you do have. It is offensive to God because you are ignoring all he has already blessed you with instead of being grateful for it.

JAMES 4:11 | *Don't speak evil against each other, dear brothers and sisters.*

Complaining about others often leads to gossip and slander, and it usually leads you to say things about them you may later regret.

When I complain, what does it say about me?

DEUTERONOMY 1:27-28 | *You complained in your tents and said, "The LORD must hate us. . . . Where can we go?"*

Complaining demonstrates an ungrateful and selfish heart. It shows a lack of gratitude for what God has given you. It also shows a lack of trust in him to care for you. When you complain, you are actually grumbling about God!

What effect does my complaining have on others?

NEHEMIAH 5:6 | *When [Nehemiah] heard their complaints, [he] was very angry.*

Those who must listen to constant complaining find it very irritating. No one likes to be around a complainer.

What should I do instead of complaining?

EPHESIANS 4:29 | *Let everything you say be good and helpful, so that your words will be an encouragement to those who hear them.*

PHILIPPIANS 2:14-15 | *Do everything without complaining and arguing, so that no one can criticize you.*

Instead of complaining, say something nice. If you can't do that, then don't say anything at all. At least if you're quiet, you can't be blamed for being negative.

LAMENTATIONS 3:39-40 | *Why should we, mere humans, complain when we are punished for our sins? Instead, let us test and examine our ways. Let us turn back to the LORD.*

Instead of complaining about the sins of others, take a look at your own sins and repent of them.

LUKE 6:37 | *Do not judge others, and you will not be judged. Do not condemn others, or it will all come back against you. Forgive others, and you will be forgiven.*

Instead of complaining about the weaknesses or wrong-doing of others, forgive them as you would like to be forgiven.

Promise from God 2 CORINTHIANS 13:11 | *Encourage each other. Live in harmony and peace. Then the God of love and peace will be with you.*

COMPROMISE

What is the difference between compromising and negotiating?

DANIEL 1:8 | *Daniel was determined not to defile himself by eating the food and wine given to them by the king. He asked the chief of staff for permission not to eat these unacceptable foods.*

Both compromise and negotiation involve a settlement of differences between parties by mutual consent. Compromising and negotiating can have the same end goal—the greatest good for all parties involved. But another meaning of compromise is to make a concession to something derogatory—to give in instead of standing up for one's principles. Daniel was able to negotiate a settlement without compromising his convictions, so that both the king and Daniel got what they wanted. When you must negotiate, never compromise your Christian convictions.

When is compromise appropriate?

PHILIPPIANS 2:2 | *Make me truly happy by agreeing whole-heartedly with each other, loving one another, and working together with one mind and purpose.*

Sometimes you need to compromise for the sake of unity in the church. Reaching an agreement may mean giving up something you want for the sake of what is best for everyone.

ROMANS 14:15 | *If another believer is distressed by what you eat, you are not acting in love if you eat it. Don't let your eating ruin someone for whom Christ died.*

ROMANS 15:1 | *We who are strong must be considerate of those who are sensitive about things like this. We must not just please ourselves.*

Sometimes you must compromise so you don't offend others or cause them to stumble in their faith. This may require you to compromise your personal preferences. However, you are never required to compromise essential Christian beliefs.

When is compromise inappropriate?

ROMANS 6:12 | *Do not let sin control the way you live; do not give in to sinful desires.*

Compromise is inappropriate when it causes you to sin in any way.

EXODUS 23:2 | *You must not follow the crowd in doing wrong.*

1 SAMUEL 15:24 | *Saul admitted to Samuel, "Yes, I have sinned. I have disobeyed your instructions and the LORD's command, for I was afraid of the people and did what they demanded."*

3 JOHN 1:11 | *Dear friend, don't let this bad example influence you. Follow only what is good.*

Compromise is inappropriate when it is motivated by peer pressure or the bad example of others.

Promise from God 1 CHRONICLES 22:13 | *You will be successful if you carefully obey the decrees and regulations that the LORD gave to Israel through Moses. Be strong and courageous; do not be afraid or lose heart!*

CONFESSION

What is involved in true confession?

PSALM 38:18 | *I confess my sins; I am deeply sorry for what I have done.*

PSALM 51:3-4, 6, 17 | *I recognize my rebellion; it haunts me day and night. Against you, and you alone, have I sinned; I have done what is evil in your sight. . . . But you desire honesty from the womb, teaching me wisdom even there. . . . The sacrifice you desire is a broken spirit. You will not reject a broken and repentant heart, O God.*

Sorrowing over your sin, humbly seeking God and his forgiveness, turning to God in prayer, turning away from sin—these are the ingredients of true confession.

To whom do I need to confess?

1 CHRONICLES 21:8 | *David said to God, "I have sinned greatly by taking this census. Please forgive my guilt for doing this foolish thing."*

EZRA 10:11 | *Confess your sin to the LORD, the God of your ancestors, and do what he demands.*

PSALM 41:4 | *"O LORD," I prayed, "have mercy on me. Heal me, for I have sinned against you."*

You must confess your sins to God because all sin is ultimately against him.

NUMBERS 5:6-7 | *If any of the people—men or women—betray the LORD by doing wrong to another person, they are guilty. They must confess their sin and make full restitution for what they have done, adding an additional 20 percent and returning it to the person who was wronged.*

JAMES 5:16 | *Confess your sins to each other and pray for each other so that you may be healed.*

You must confess your sins to others when you have wronged them and need their forgiveness.

Does God's forgiveness always follow true confession?

PSALM 32:5 | *I confessed all my sins to you and stopped trying to hide my guilt. . . . And you forgave me! All my guilt is gone.*

PSALM 65:3 | *Though we are overwhelmed by our sins, you forgive them all.*

PSALM 86:5 | *O Lord, you are so good, so ready to forgive, so full of unfailing love for all who ask for your help.*

God's supply of forgiveness far exceeds the number of times you could ever go to him for forgiveness.

Promise from God 1 JOHN 1:9 | *If we confess our sins to him, he is faithful and just to forgive us our sins and to cleanse us from all wickedness.*

CONFLICT/CONFRONTATION

What causes conflict?

PROVERBS 13:10 | *Pride leads to conflict.*

PROVERBS 28:25 | *Greed causes fighting.*

PROVERBS 30:33 | *As the beating of cream yields butter and striking the nose causes bleeding, so stirring up anger causes quarrels.*

JAMES 4:1 | *What is causing the quarrels and fights among you? Don't they come from the evil desires at war within you?*

There are many causes of conflict between people, but pride, greed, and anger are prime offenders. Our sinful human nature sows the seeds of most conflict.

ROMANS 7:22-23 | *I love God's law with all my heart. But there is another power within me that is at war with my mind. This power makes me a slave to the sin that is still within me.*

Those who follow Christ also experience conflict within themselves between their old sinful nature and their new spiritual nature.

What are some ways to resolve conflict?

1 CORINTHIANS 6:7 | *Even to have such lawsuits with one another is a defeat for you. Why not just accept the injustice and leave it at that? Why not let yourselves be cheated?*

You might have to give up your rights in order to resolve a conflict of interests.

JOHN 17:21 | *I pray that they will all be one, just as you and I are one—as you are in me, Father, and I am in you.*

Praying for peace and unity makes a difference because you are seeking the help of the Prince of Peace.

2 TIMOTHY 2:24-25 | *A servant of the Lord must not quarrel but must be kind to everyone, be able to teach, and be patient with difficult people. Gently instruct those who oppose the truth.*

When someone disagrees with you, maintain a gracious, gentle, and patient attitude instead of becoming angry and defensive.

Under what circumstances is confrontation necessary?

EPHESIANS 5:11 | *Take no part in the worthless deeds of evil and darkness; instead, expose them.*

Evil and wickedness must be confronted or they may consume you.

PROVERBS 27:5 | *An open rebuke is better than hidden love!*

LUKE 17:3 | *If another believer sins, rebuke that person; then if there is repentance, forgive.*

You should confront someone who does wrong, with the goal of reconciling that person to God and others.

How can I effectively confront others?

MATTHEW 18:15-17 | *If another believer sins against you, go privately and point out the offense. If the other person listens and confesses it, you have won that person back. But if you are unsuccessful, take one or two others with you and go back again, so that everything you say may be confirmed by two or three witnesses. If the person still refuses to listen, take your case to the church. Then if he or she won't accept the church's decision, treat that person as a pagan or a corrupt tax collector.*

Go to the person and confront him or her in private. If he or she does not listen, go with another concerned friend. If the person still refuses to listen, take the matter to the spiritual leaders of your church for guidance and advice.

2 TIMOTHY 1:7 | *God has not given us a spirit of fear and timidity, but of power, love, and self-discipline.*

Confront others in power and love, making sure that you are acting from a spirit that has first applied self-discipline.

Promise from God MATTHEW 5:9 | *God blesses those who work for peace, for they will be called the children of God.*

CONSEQUENCES

—•●

What are the consequences of sin?

EZEKIEL 3:20 | *If righteous people turn away from their righteous behavior and ignore the obstacles I put in their way, they will die.*

ROMANS 6:23 | *The wages of sin is death.*

The greatest consequence of sin is death, which leads to eternal separation from God.

GENESIS 3:17 | *To the man [God] said, "Since you listened to your wife and ate from the tree whose fruit I commanded you not to eat, the ground is cursed because of you. All your life you will struggle to scratch a living from it."*

Hardship and difficulty are consequences of sin.

JEREMIAH 11:8 | *Your ancestors did not listen or even pay attention. Instead, they stubbornly followed their own evil desires. And because they refused to obey, I brought upon them all the curses described in this covenant.*

Sin invites the full impact of God's warnings, which often includes his punishment. Sometimes God's punishment is immediate, and sometimes he delays it.

PSALM 7:14-16 | *The wicked conceive evil. . . . They dig a deep pit to trap others, then fall into it themselves. The trouble they make for others backfires on them. The violence they plan falls on their own heads.*

Any evil you plan for others may come back to destroy you.

PROVERBS 18:21 | *The tongue can bring death or life; those who love to talk will reap the consequences.*

Harmful words you speak against someone else may come back to condemn you.

Do I ever suffer the consequences of another person's sin?

JOSHUA 7:25 | *Joshua said to Achan, "Why have you brought trouble on us?"*

Sin always affects others. You live in a sinful world. You suffer from the sins of your parents and others around you. It is wise, then, to remember that your own sinful actions don't affect just yourself. Beware of the temptation to rationalize your sins, telling yourself they are too small or too personal to hurt anyone.

EZEKIEL 3:20 | *If righteous people turn away from their righteous behavior . . ., they will die. And if you do not warn them, they will die in their sins. None of their righteous acts will be remembered, and I will hold you responsible for their deaths.*

You suffer the consequences of another person's sin—guilt before God—if you remain silent when you should have warned that person of the consequences of his or her actions.

ROMANS 5:12 | *Adam's sin brought death, so death spread to everyone, for everyone sinned.*

Everyone still suffers the consequences of Adam's sin, but you, too, have sinned and deserve the same punishment as Adam.

EZEKIEL 18:20 | *The person who sins is the one who will die.*

While you may suffer the consequences of another person's sins, be assured that the one who sins against you will also reap the consequences.

Promise from God HOSEA 10:12 | *Plant the good seeds of righteousness, and you will harvest a crop of love. Plow up the hard ground of your hearts, for now is the time to seek the LORD, that he may come and shower righteousness upon you.*

CONTENTMENT

How can I find contentment regardless of life's circumstances?

2 CORINTHIANS 12:10 | *That's why I take pleasure in my weaknesses, and in the insults, hardships, persecutions, and troubles that I suffer for Christ. For when I am weak, then I am strong.*

PHILIPPIANS 4:11-13 | *I have learned how to be content with whatever I have. I know how to live on almost nothing or with everything. I have learned the secret of living in every situation, whether it is with a full stomach or empty, with plenty or little. For I can do everything through Christ, who gives me strength.*

2 PETER 1:3 | *By his divine power, God has given us everything we need for living a godly life. We have received all of this by coming to know him, the one who called us to himself by means of his marvelous glory and excellence.*

When you depend on circumstances for your contentment, you become unhappy when things don't go your way. When you depend on Jesus for your contentment, you are secure because he will never fail you.

What is the relationship between wealth and contentment?

ECCLESIASTES 5:10 | *Those who love money will never have enough. How meaningless to think that wealth brings true happiness!*

1 TIMOTHY 6:17 | *Teach those who are rich in this world not to be proud and not to trust in their money, which is so unreliable. Their trust should be in God, who richly gives us all we need for our enjoyment.*

If you think that having "just a little" more money will bring you contentment, you are deceived. No amount of wealth can bring contentment. True contentment comes from knowing you are loved by God and from serving others.

ECCLESIASTES 5:19-20 | *To enjoy your work and accept your lot in life—this is indeed a gift from God. God keeps such people so busy enjoying life that they take no time to brood over the past.*

HEBREWS 13:5 | *Don't love money; be satisfied with what you have. For God has said, "I will never fail you. I will never abandon you."*

Contentment is not dependent on wealth, nor does it have to be stifled by poverty. Wealth by itself is neutral—neither good nor bad. Contentment is not related to how many things you have but how much of God you have. The key is to thank God for what you have and to use your time and resources to please him.

1 TIMOTHY 6:6-7 | *True godliness with contentment is itself great wealth. After all, we brought nothing with us when we came into the world, and we can't take anything with us when we leave it.*

Knowing that your real home is in heaven with God should help you find contentment because your future is secure. Making wise personal investments of your time, your character, and your relationships here on earth will bring you great wealth in heaven.

Promise from God 2 PETER 1:3 | *By his divine power, God has given us everything we need for living a godly life. We have received all of this by coming to know him, the one who called us to himself by means of his marvelous glory and excellence.*

CRISIS

What are some possible causes of crisis in my life?

JONAH 1:4, 12 | *The LORD hurled a powerful wind over the sea, causing a violent storm that threatened to break the ship apart. . . . "Throw me into the sea," Jonah said, "and it will become calm again. I know that this terrible storm is all my fault."*

Jonah was in crisis because he ran away from God, but the sailors were in crisis, too, because of Jonah's sin! You can cause a crisis for others by your sin, or your crisis could be the result of someone else's sin.

PROVERBS 27:12 | *A prudent person foresees danger and takes precautions. The simpleton goes blindly on and suffers the consequences.*

Sometimes a crisis is the result of poor decisions.

ECCLESIASTES 9:12 | *People can never predict when hard times might come. Like fish in a net or birds in a trap, people are caught by sudden tragedy.*

Sometimes a crisis comes for no apparent reason. It's no one's fault—just a part of living in this fallen world.

JOB 36:15 | *By means of their suffering, [God] rescues those who suffer. For he gets their attention through adversity.*

Sometimes God allows a crisis in your life to get your attention.

2 CORINTHIANS 4:11 | *Yes, we live under constant danger of death because we serve Jesus, so that the life of Jesus will be evident in our dying bodies.*

Sometimes a crisis comes because you serve Jesus, and serving Jesus can bring persecution.

Can blessings come from my times of crisis?

JONAH 1:16 | *The sailors were awestruck by the LORD's great power, and they offered him a sacrifice and vowed to serve him.*

Sometimes a crisis helps you see God more clearly.

PHILIPPIANS 1:12 | *I want you to know, my dear brothers and sisters, that everything that has happened to me here has helped to spread the Good News.*

How you react to times of crisis can influence what others think about Christ.

ROMANS 5:3-4 | *We can rejoice, too, when we run into problems and trials, for we know that they help us develop endurance. And endurance develops strength of character, and character strengthens our confident hope of salvation.*

Times of crisis can strengthen your character.

1 PETER 4:13 | *Be very glad—for these trials make you partners with Christ in his suffering.*

Times of crisis help you identify with the suffering that Jesus endured for your sake.

How should I respond to crisis?

PSALM 57:1 | *Have mercy on me, O God, have mercy! I look to you for protection. I will hide beneath the shadow of your wings until the danger passes by.*

PSALM 130:1-2 | *From the depths of despair, O LORD, I call for your help. Hear my cry, O Lord. Pay attention to my prayer.*

When you reach the end of your rope, call upon the Lord. Your times of weakness are his times for strength; your crises are his opportunities.

PSALM 119:143 | *As pressure and stress bear down on me, I find joy in your commands.*

When a crisis threatens to overwhelm you, God's Word is a firm foundation to keep you from falling into a bottomless pit.

Promise from God   PSALM 46:1 | *God is our refuge and strength, always ready to help in times of trouble.*

CRITICISM

How should I respond to criticism?

PROVERBS 12:16-18 | *A fool is quick-tempered, but a wise person stays calm when insulted. An honest witness tells the truth; a false witness tells lies. Some people make cutting remarks, but the words of the wise bring healing.*

If you are criticized, stay calm and don't lash back. Evaluate whether the criticism comes from a person who is telling the truth or might be telling lies. Ask yourself if the criticism is meant to heal or to hurt.

ECCLESIASTES 7:5 | *Better to be criticized by a wise person than to be praised by a fool.*

Measure the criticism according to the character of the person who is giving it.

1 CORINTHIANS 4:4 | *My conscience is clear, but that doesn't prove I'm right. It is the Lord himself who will examine me and decide.*

Keep your conscience clear by being honest and trustworthy. This helps you shrug off criticism that you know is unjustified.

1 PETER 4:14 | *Be happy when you are insulted for being a Christian, for then the glorious Spirit of God rests upon you.*

Consider it a privilege to be criticized for your faith in God. God has special blessings for those who patiently endure this kind of criticism.

Why should I be careful about criticizing others?

ROMANS 14:10 | *Why do you condemn another believer? Why do you look down on another believer? Remember, we will all stand before the judgment seat of God.*

JAMES 4:11 | *Don't speak evil against each other, dear brothers and sisters. If you criticize and judge each other, then you are criticizing and judging God's law.*

Constructive criticism can be a welcome and wholesome gift if it is given in a spirit of love. But criticism that ridicules, demeans, or judges people has at least four harmful consequences: (1) It tears down self-esteem, making the recipients feel shamed and worthless; (2) it damages your reputation, making you look mean and merciless; (3) it damages your ability to offer helpful advice because you've made people defensive; and (4) it brings judgment upon you from God, who detests it when you hurt others.

Promise from God ROMANS 14:17-18 | *The Kingdom of God is . . . living a life of goodness and peace and joy in the Holy Spirit. If you serve Christ with this attitude, you will please God, and others will approve of you, too.*

DEATH

What will happen to me when I die?

1 CORINTHIANS 15:52 | *When the trumpet sounds, those who have died will be raised to live forever. And we who are living will also be transformed.*

1 THESSALONIANS 4:13 | *Dear brothers and sisters, we want you to know what will happen to the believers who have died so you will not grieve like people who have no hope.*

REVELATION 14:11 | *The smoke of their torment will rise forever and ever, and they will have no relief day or night, for they have worshiped the beast and his statue and have accepted the mark of his name.*

REVELATION 20:15 | *Anyone whose name was not found recorded in the Book of Life was thrown into the lake of fire.*

REVELATION 21:3 | *Look, God's home is now among his people!*

What an adventure awaits those who love Jesus Christ! A Christian who dies will meet God and live with him forever in heaven. Our bodies will be totally transformed into bodies that will never again be subjected to sin, pain, and the limitations of this world.

How do I keep a proper perspective about death? Why am I afraid of it?

PHILIPPIANS 1:21 | *To me, living means living for Christ, and dying is even better.*

Fear of dying may be an indication of a weak relationship with God, a misunderstanding of heaven, a lack of the proper perspective that what you do here affects how you live there, or a lack of trust in God's promises. When you are at peace with God, you will not fear death.

2 CORINTHIANS 5:4 | *While we live in these earthly bodies, we groan and sigh, but it's not that we want to die and get rid of these bodies that clothe us. Rather, we want to put on our new bodies so that these dying bodies will be swallowed up by life.*

COLOSSIANS 3:1-2 | *Since you have been raised to new life with Christ, set your sights on the realities of heaven. . . . Think about the things of heaven, not the things of earth.*

Fear of the unknown is natural, but fear of death can be useful when it draws you closer to God and causes you to make every day count for him. Spend time realizing that death is a beginning, not the end—it is your entrance into eternal life with God. And learning what the Bible says about heaven will make you look forward to being there.

In life after death, will I keep my body or get a new one or have no body at all?

1 CORINTHIANS 15:42 | *Our earthly bodies are planted in the ground when we die, but they will be raised to live forever.*

You will have a body—the Bible clearly teaches that you will not be just a spirit floating around. But you really wouldn't want to live in your present body forever. It gets sick and increasingly becomes a burden to you; it ages and deteriorates. Think of how many problems your body would accumulate over a few thousand years! Instead, you will welcome the new body God gives you, realizing how healthy and amazing it will be compared to your present one.

Promise from God JOHN 11:25 | *Jesus [said], "I am the resurrection and the life. Anyone who believes in me will live, even after dying."*

DECEIT

What does God think of lying and other forms of deception?

PSALM 5:6 | *You will destroy those who tell lies. The LORD detests murderers and deceivers.*

PROVERBS 6:16-17, 19 | *There are six things the LORD hates— no, seven things he detests: haughty eyes, a lying tongue, . . . a false witness who pours out lies.*

God hates deception and lying.

PSALM 101:7 | *I will not allow deceivers to serve in my house, and liars will not stay in my presence.*

ISAIAH 59:2-3 | *It's your sins that have cut you off from God. . . . Your lips are full of lies, and your mouth spews corruption.*

Deceit creates a barrier between you and God.

ZEPHANIAH 3:13 | *The remnant of Israel will do no wrong; they will never tell lies or deceive one another. They will eat and sleep in safety, and no one will make them afraid.*

Those who practice honesty in obedience to God can count on blessings from God.

Is deception always wrong?

LEVITICUS 19:11 | *Do not steal. Do not deceive or cheat one another.*

PROVERBS 24:28 | *Don't testify against your neighbors without cause; don't lie about them.*

COLOSSIANS 3:9 | *Don't lie to each other, for you have stripped off your old sinful nature and all its wicked deeds.*

God has commanded you not to lie or be involved in deception.

REVELATION 21:8 | *Cowards, unbelievers, the corrupt, murderers, the immoral, those who practice witchcraft, idol worshipers, and all liars—their fate is in the fiery lake of burning sulfur. This is the second death.*

REVELATION 21:27 | *Nothing evil will be allowed to enter, nor anyone who practices shameful idolatry and dishonesty—but only those whose names are written in the Lamb's Book of Life.*

The Bible makes it clear that deception is a sin.

Promise from God PSALM 32:2 | *What joy for those whose record the LORD has cleared of guilt, whose lives are lived in complete honesty!*

DENIAL

What does it mean to deny God?

ROMANS 1:21 | *Yes, they knew God, but they wouldn't worship him as God or even give him thanks.*

1 JOHN 2:22-23 | *Who is a liar? Anyone who says that Jesus is not the Christ. Anyone who denies the Father and the Son is an antichrist. Anyone who denies the Son doesn't have the Father, either.*

To refuse to acknowledge God's authority or your need for Jesus to save you is to deny him.

MATTHEW 26:69-70 | *"You were one of those with Jesus the Galilean." But Peter denied it in front of everyone. "I don't know what you're talking about," he said.*

To be ashamed of Jesus is to deny him.

TITUS 1:16 | *Such people claim they know God, but they deny him by the way they live. They are detestable and disobedient, worthless for doing anything good.*

You deny God if you say you know him but then live as though you don't.

What are the consequences of denying God?

ROMANS 1:28 | *Since they thought it foolish to acknowledge God, he abandoned them to their foolish thinking and let them do things that should never be done.*

People who deny God end up becoming increasingly evil.

MATTHEW 10:32-33 | *Everyone who denies me here on earth, I will also deny before my Father in heaven.*

2 TIMOTHY 2:12 | *If we deny him, he will deny us.*

Those who deny Jesus face the awful consequence of having Jesus deny them on the Day of Judgment.

What kinds of self-denial does God call me to?

GALATIANS 5:24 | *Those who belong to Christ Jesus have nailed the passions and desires of their sinful nature to his cross and crucified them there.*

God calls you to exercise restraint and self-discipline in the way you live.

LUKE 14:33 | *You cannot become my disciple without giving up everything you own.*

PHILIPPIANS 3:8 | *Yes, everything else is worthless when compared with the infinite value of knowing Christ Jesus my Lord. For his sake I have discarded everything else, counting it all as garbage, so that I could gain Christ.*

If you were asked, would you be willing to give up everything for Jesus? He may not ask you to do something that dramatic, but he loves that kind of attitude in his followers.

Promise from God LUKE 18:29-30 | *Jesus [said], "I assure you that everyone who has given up house or wife or brothers or parents or children, for the sake of the Kingdom of God, will be repaid many times over in this life, and will have eternal life in the world to come."*

DESIRES

Is it okay to want something?

1 KINGS 3:5 | *That night the LORD appeared to Solomon in a dream, and God said, "What do you want? Ask, and I will give it to you!"*

PROVERBS 13:12 | *Hope deferred makes the heart sick, but a dream fulfilled is a tree of life.*

God created desire within you as a means of expressing yourself. Desire is healthy if it is directed toward the proper objects: those that are right and good and God honoring.

PSALM 73:25 | *I desire you more than anything on earth.*

ISAIAH 26:8 | *LORD, we show our trust in you by obeying your laws; our heart's desire is to glorify your name.*

JEREMIAH 29:13 | *If you look for me wholeheartedly, you will find me.*

Your greatest desire must be a relationship with God. That will influence all your other desires.

ROMANS 6:12 | *Do not let sin control the way you live; do not give in to sinful desires.*

Make sure the object of your desire is pure, consistent with God's Word, and not harmful to others.

How do I resist evil desires?

JAMES 3:13 | *If you are wise and understand God's ways, prove it by living an honorable life, doing good works with the humility that comes from wisdom.*

Keep yourself busy doing good.

MATTHEW 6:13 | *Don't let us yield to temptation, but rescue us from the evil one.*

Pray that good desires will take the place of bad ones.

2 CHRONICLES 34:33 | *Josiah removed all detestable idols from the entire land of Israel and required everyone to worship the LORD their God.*

Avoid the source of temptation.

PHILIPPIANS 4:8 | *Fix your thoughts on what is true, and honorable, and right, and pure, and lovely, and admirable. Think about things that are excellent and worthy of praise.*

COLOSSIANS 3:2 | *Think about the things of heaven, not the things of earth.*

Fill your mind with God and thoughts that honor him.

PROVERBS 15:22 | *Plans go wrong for lack of advice; many advisers bring success.*

Find a person who will hold you accountable.

Can God help me change the desires of my heart? How?

ROMANS 7:6 | *Now we can serve God, not in the old way . . . but in the new way of living in the Spirit.*

When you give control of your life to God, he gives you a new heart, a new nature, and a new desire to please him.

EZRA 1:5 | *God stirred the hearts of the priests and Levites . . . to rebuild the Temple of the LORD.*

God stirs your heart with right desires. It is up to you to act upon them.

Promise from God PSALM 37:4 | *Take delight in the LORD, and he will give you your heart's desires.*

DIFFERENCES

How does God want me to handle differences with others?

PSALM 133:1-3 | *How wonderful and pleasant it is when brothers live together in harmony! For harmony is as precious as the anointing oil. . . . Harmony is as refreshing as the dew. . . . The LORD has pronounced his blessing, even life everlasting.*

Live in harmony despite your differences. In the church, God wants you to function together in unity. When Christians accept their differences and produce harmony, the church becomes a healing and refreshing balm to the community.

PROVERBS 17:14 | *Starting a quarrel is like opening a floodgate, so stop before a dispute breaks out.*

1 CORINTHIANS 1:10 | *I appeal to you, dear brothers and sisters, by the authority of our Lord Jesus Christ, to live in harmony with each other. Let there be no divisions in the church. Rather, be of one mind, united in thought and purpose.*

Arguing over differences of opinion usually does more harm than good. Instead, talk about how your differences can become part of the solution. This helps everyone be more productive, and it promotes peace.

EPHESIANS 2:14 | *Christ himself has brought peace to us. He united Jews and Gentiles into one people when, in his own body on the cross, he broke down the wall of hostility that separated us.*

Christ has broken down the wall of hostility that used to separate you from others. Therefore, do all you can to avoid hostility between you.

EPHESIANS 4:3 | *Make every effort to keep yourselves united in the Spirit, binding yourselves together with peace.*

God has brought together very different people in the church, and he unites them through the Holy Spirit. So, when disagreements happen, work to dissolve them in order to maintain unity in the church.

Can my differences with others help me be stronger?

PROVERBS 27:17 | *As iron sharpens iron, so a friend sharpens a friend.*

ROMANS 12:5 | *So it is with Christ's body. We are many parts of one body, and we all belong to each other.*

Just as all kinds of instruments strengthen an orchestra, so people with different gifts and perspectives make any group stronger. God often brings very different people together in marriage, too, so that their gifts can complement each other. Ironically, it is usually through diversity that the most progress is made. If everyone always thought the same way, the status quo would never change and little would get done.

Promise from God 2 CORINTHIANS 13:11 | *Live in harmony and peace. Then the God of love and peace will be with you.*

DIVORCE

What does the Bible say about divorce?

MALACHI 2:14-16 | *You cry out, "Why doesn't the LORD accept my worship?" I'll tell you why! Because the LORD witnessed the vows you and your wife made when you were young. But you have been unfaithful to her. . . . Didn't the LORD make you one with your wife? In body and spirit you are his. . . . So guard your heart; remain loyal to the wife of your youth. "For I hate divorce!" says the LORD, the God of Israel.*

The Bible says divorce is wrong because it is breaking a binding commitment a man and a woman made before God at their wedding. It is tearing apart what God had bound together into one seamless piece. Divorce is the conscious decision by one or both mates to break this sacred commitment.

MATTHEW 19:3 | *Some Pharisees came and tried to trap him with this question: "Should a man be allowed to divorce his wife for just any reason?"*

Both the Old and New Testaments acknowledge the reality of divorce. Even among believers today, divorce happens, despite good intentions and efforts. The fact remains that divorce is wrong, just as any sin is wrong. But another fact is also clear: Any sin can be forgiven. You do not have to forfeit joy and blessing for the rest of your life. God restores sinners, no matter how great their sin. So while God clearly says in the Bible that divorce is sin, he also clearly explains how to be forgiven and how to restore your relationship with him and make peace with your wife, even if your marriage cannot be salvaged. Be careful, however, not to use God's grace as a loophole for divorce.

What are some ways to prevent divorce?

EPHESIANS 5:24-25 | *As the church submits to Christ, so you wives should submit to your husbands in everything. For husbands, this means love your wives, just as Christ loved the church. He gave up his life for her.*

1 THESSALONIANS 5:11 | *Encourage each other and build each other up, just as you are already doing.*

Couples who love each other with the kind of love Christ showed when he died for us, who seek to please each other, and who encourage each other and build each other up are the couples who will likely remain together in a happy marriage. The format is simple, but the fulfillment takes some doing! Don't let anyone convince you that love is easy. Sin is easy; love is hard work because it requires you to think more of your wife than yourself. But loving and serving her will bring far greater rewards than living just for yourself would.

Promise from God MATTHEW 19:6 | *Since they are no longer two but one, let no one split apart what God has joined together.*

EMPLOYERS/EMPLOYEES

How should employers treat employees?

LEVITICUS 19:13 | *Do not make your hired workers wait until the next day to receive their pay.*

DEUTERONOMY 24:14-15 | *Never take advantage of poor and destitute laborers. . . . You must pay them their wages. . . . If you don't, they might cry out to the LORD against you, and it would be counted against you as sin.*

JAMES 5:4 | *Hear the cries of the field workers whom you have cheated of their pay. The wages you held back cry out against you. The cries of those who harvest your fields have reached the ears of the LORD of Heaven's Armies.*

Employers should always pay employees promptly and should pay fair wages. God is fair and expects fairness from people.

RUTH 2:4 | *While she was there, Boaz arrived from Bethlehem and greeted the harvesters. "The LORD be with you!" he said. "The LORD bless you!" the harvesters replied.*

Employers should bless their employees by encouraging them and showing appreciation for the work they are doing.

How should employees respond to their employers?

2 KINGS 12:15 | *No accounting of this money was required from the construction supervisors, because they were honest and trustworthy men.*

PROVERBS 25:13 | *Trustworthy messengers refresh like snow in summer. They revive the spirit of their employer.*

LUKE 16:10 | *If you are faithful in little things, you will be faithful in large ones.*

Employees should be completely faithful and honest in their work.

PROVERBS 10:26 | *Lazy people irritate their employers, like vinegar to the teeth or smoke in the eyes.*

Employees should work hard for their employers.

ECCLESIASTES 10:4 | *If your boss is angry at you, don't quit! A quiet spirit can overcome even great mistakes.*

Even if an employer is critical and overbearing, employees should continue to do their best and strive to please God.

LUKE 3:14 | *"What should we do?" asked some soldiers. John replied, "Don't extort money or make false accusations. And be content with your pay."*

Employees should learn to be content with their wages and not try to get more by cheating.

Promise from God PROVERBS 27:18 | *As workers who tend a fig tree are allowed to eat the fruit, so workers who protect their employer's interests will be rewarded.*

EXCUSES

Why do I sometimes make excuses for the wrong things I do?

EXODUS 4:10 | *Moses pleaded with the LORD, "O Lord, I'm not very good with words. I never have been, and I'm not now, even though you have spoken to me. I get tongue-tied, and my words get tangled."*

NUMBERS 13:31 | *The other men who had explored the land with him disagreed. "We can't go up against them! They are stronger than we are!"*

JUDGES 6:15 | *"But Lord," Gideon replied, "how can I rescue Israel? My clan is the weakest in the whole tribe of Manasseh, and I am the least in my entire family!"*

Lack of self-confidence, which can also be a lack of confidence in God, is often a reason for resisting what God wants you to do.

GENESIS 4:9 | *The LORD asked Cain, "Where is your brother? Where is Abel?" "I don't know," Cain responded. "Am I my brother's guardian?"*

Excuses are often an attempt to cover up the wrong you have done.

1 SAMUEL 13:12 | *"I [Saul] said, 'The Philistines are ready to march against us at Gilgal, and I haven't even asked for the LORD's help!' So I felt compelled to offer the burnt offering myself before you came."*

Sometimes I make excuses because I want to appear pious.

PROVERBS 22:13 | *The lazy person claims, "There's a lion out there! If I go outside, I might be killed!"*

Laziness is at the root of some excuses.

LUKE 9:59, 61 | *[Jesus] said to another person, "Come, follow me." The man agreed, but he said, "Lord, first let me return home and bury my father." . . . Another said, "Yes, Lord, I will follow you, but first let me say good-bye to my family."*

I sometimes make excuses to cover up a lack of commitment.

How does God respond when I make excuses for my sin?

1 SAMUEL 15:22 | *What is more pleasing to the LORD: your burnt offerings and sacrifices or your obedience to his voice? Listen! Obedience is better than sacrifice, and submission is better than offering the fat of rams.*

God sees through attempts to excuse sin. He wants obedience, not excuses for disobedience.

GENESIS 4:10-11 | *The LORD said, "What have you done? Listen! Your brother's blood cries out to me from the ground! Now you are cursed and banished from the ground, which has swallowed your brother's blood."*

Excusing sin will not be overlooked by God. You can't hide from him, so don't bother trying. You would only be setting yourself up for future judgment.

Promise from God 1 JOHN 1:8-9 | *If we claim we have no sin, we are only fooling ourselves and not living in the truth. But if we confess our sins to him, he is faithful and just to forgive us our sins and to cleanse us from all wickedness.*

EXPECTATIONS

What can I look forward to?

PROVERBS 11:23 | *The godly can look forward to a reward, while the wicked can expect only judgment.*

ROMANS 5:4-5 | *Character strengthens our confident hope of salvation. And this hope will not lead to disappointment.*

2 CORINTHIANS 3:8 | *Shouldn't we expect far greater glory under the new way, now that the Holy Spirit is giving life?*

HEBREWS 10:26-27 | *Dear friends, if we deliberately continue sinning after we have received knowledge of the truth, there is no longer any sacrifice that will cover these sins. There is only the terrible expectation of God's judgment and the raging fire that will consume his enemies.*

Those who trust in Christ for salvation can expect eternal life with God. Those who rebel against God can expect his judgment.

What are some unrealistic expectations?

EZEKIEL 44:12 | *They encouraged my people to worship idols, causing Israel to fall into deep sin. So I have taken a solemn oath that they must bear the consequences for their sins, says the Sovereign LORD.*

GALATIANS 6:7 | *You will always harvest what you plant.*

You should not expect that you can live sinfully and never suffer the consequences.

ECCLESIASTES 10:8-9 | *When you dig a well, you might fall in. When you demolish an old wall, you could be bitten by a snake. When you work in a quarry, stones might fall and crush you. When you chop wood, there is danger with each stroke of your ax.*

You should not expect life to be free from danger and risk.

2 CORINTHIANS 11:7 | *Was I wrong when I humbled myself and honored you by preaching God's Good News to you without expecting anything in return?*

You should not expect to be rewarded by others for serving God and obeying him.

LUKE 13:26-27 | *You will say, "But we ate and drank with you, and you taught in our streets." And he will reply, "I tell you, I don't know you or where you come from. Get away from me, all you who do evil."*

You should not expect to get into heaven by merely knowing *about* Christ. You must know him personally and trust in him for forgiveness and eternal life.

Promise from God 1 PETER 1:3-4 | *We live with great expectation, and we have a priceless inheritance—an inheritance that is kept in heaven for you, pure and undefiled, beyond the reach of change and decay.*

FAILURE

How can I avoid failure?

MATTHEW 7:24-27 | *[Jesus said,] "Anyone who listens to my teaching and follows it is wise, like a person who builds a house on solid rock. Though the rain comes in torrents and the floodwaters rise and the winds beat against that house, it won't collapse because it is built on bedrock. But anyone who hears my teaching and doesn't obey it is foolish, like a person who builds a house on sand. When the rains and floods come and the winds beat against that house, it will collapse with a mighty crash."*

Failure results when you ignore God's voice and disobey his Word. The Bible is God's instruction manual for how life really works. It is the foundation that keeps your life from falling apart. You can often prevent failure by reading the Bible and building your life on its principles.

MATTHEW 16:26 | *What do you benefit if you gain the whole world but lose your own soul? Is anything worth more than your soul?*

If you managed a successful business, raised a good family, won all kinds of community awards, and retired comfortably, would you say your life had been a success? God says it would have been a failure if you did all this apart from him. Don't fail by neglecting or ignoring God. Don't fail to discover what a relationship with God means for your present and your future.

JOSHUA 8:1 | *The LORD said to Joshua, "Do not be afraid or discouraged."*

Giving up is a sure way to fail. Courage and perseverance help prevent failure, especially if you know that God approves of the task you are doing.

ISAIAH 42:23 | *Who will hear these lessons from the past and see the ruin that awaits you in the future?*

You can avoid failure by learning from the mistakes of the past.

PROVERBS 15:22 | *Plans go wrong for lack of advice; many advisers bring success.*

Good advice helps prevent failure. A concert of wise counsel makes good music for success.

What must I learn about failure?

GENESIS 3:12-13 | *The man replied, "It was the woman you gave me who gave me the fruit, and I ate it." Then the LORD God asked the woman, "What have you done?" "The serpent deceived me," she replied.*

One thing is certain: You must learn to live with failure. Everyone has weaknesses. The key to recovery is not how seldom you fail but how you respond to failure. Adam and Eve, for example, responded to their failure by trying to place the blame elsewhere rather than admitting their wrongs and seeking forgiveness.

JONAH 1:3 | *Jonah got up and went in the opposite direction to get away from the LORD.*

Don't make the mistake of running away from God. It will bring the worst kind of failure.

COLOSSIANS 3:23-24 | *Work willingly at whatever you do, as though you were working for the Lord rather than for people. Remember that the Lord will give you an inheritance as your reward, and that the Master you are serving is Christ.*

Scripture reminds you to define success in terms of faithfulness to God. God will reward your faithfulness even if you fail in the eyes of the world.

Promise from God PSALM 37:23-24 | *The LORD directs the steps of the godly. He delights in every detail of their lives. Though they stumble, they will never fall, for the LORD holds them by the hand.*

FAIRNESS

What does God/the Bible say about fairness?

EXODUS 23:2-3 | *You must not follow the crowd in doing wrong. When you are called to testify in a dispute, do not be swayed by the crowd to twist justice. And do not slant your testimony in favor of a person just because that person is poor.*

LEVITICUS 19:15 | *Do not twist justice in legal matters by favoring the poor or being partial to the rich and powerful. Always judge people fairly.*

God wants you to treat people equally, as much as possible, and to judge them fairly.

ISAIAH 33:15-16 | *Those who are honest and fair, who refuse to profit by fraud, who stay far away from bribes, who refuse to listen to those who plot murder, who shut their eyes to all enticement to do wrong—these are the ones who will dwell on high.*

JEREMIAH 22:3 | *This is what the LORD says: Be fair-minded and just. Do what is right! Help those who have been robbed; rescue them from their oppressors.*

God wants you to work for justice and fairness for others.

How should I respond when life isn't fair?

ECCLESIASTES 9:11 | *The fastest runner doesn't always win the race, and the strongest warrior doesn't always win the battle. The wise sometimes go hungry, and the skillful are not necessarily wealthy.*

It is true that life is not always fair. Things don't necessarily happen the way you expected. But if you look around, you will realize that many other people are worse off than you are, so you have much to be grateful for.

EZEKIEL 18:25 | *You say, "The LORD isn't doing what's right!" Listen to me, O people of Israel. Am I the one not doing what's right, or is it you?*

Don't blame God for the unfairness of other people.

PSALM 9:8 | *He will judge the world with justice and rule the nations with fairness.*

ISAIAH 9:7 | *His government and its peace will never end. He will rule with fairness and justice from the throne of his ancestor David for all eternity.*

Recognize that right will ultimately triumph, when God takes command and rules with justice and fairness forever.

Promise from God PSALM 37:28 | *The LORD loves justice, and he will never abandon the godly. He will keep them safe forever.*

FAITH

Why should I have faith in God?

JOHN 3:16 | *God loved the world so much that he gave his one and only Son, so that everyone who believes in him will not perish but have eternal life.*

JOHN 5:24 | *[Jesus said,] "I tell you the truth, those who listen to my message and believe in God who sent me have eternal life."*

JOHN 14:6 | *I am the way, the truth, and the life. No one can come to the Father except through me.*

According to the Bible (God's own words), faith in God means believing that he sent his Son, Jesus Christ, to earth to save you from eternal death. Believing that Jesus died for your sins and rose again from the dead is the only way to receive the gift of eternal life in heaven. The One who created heaven has told you clearly how to get there.

HEBREWS 11:1 | *Faith is the confidence that what we hope for will actually happen; it gives us assurance about things we cannot see.*

Faith gives you hope. When the world seems to be a crazy, mixed-up place, believers can be absolutely confident that one day Jesus will come and make it right again. Your faith in his promise that he will do that someday will allow you to keep going today.

Faith seems so complicated; how can I find it?

MARK 5:36 | *Jesus . . . said to Jairus, "Don't be afraid. Just have faith."*

Too often we make faith too complicated. It simply means trusting Jesus to do what he has promised, and he has promised to give you life forever in heaven if you just believe he is who he said he is—the Son of God.

How much faith must I have?

MATTHEW 17:20 | *[Jesus said,] "I tell you the truth, if you had faith even as small as a mustard seed, you could say to this*

mountain, 'Move from here to there,' and it would move.
Nothing would be impossible."

The mustard seed was the smallest seed known to people
during Bible times. Jesus says that it is not the size of your
faith but the size of the One in whom you believe that
makes the difference. You do not have to have a great faith
in God; rather, you have faith in a great God.

How can I strengthen my faith?

GENESIS 12:1, 4 | *The LORD had said to Abram, "Leave your
native country . . . and go to the land that I will show you." . . .
So Abram departed as the LORD had instructed.*

Like a muscle, faith gets stronger the more you exercise it.
When you do what God asks you to do and then see him
bless you as a result of your obedience, your faith grows
even stronger.

PSALM 119:48 | *I honor and love your commands. I meditate
on your decrees.*

Faith is grounded in God's Word. Your faith will grow
stronger as you study the Bible and reflect on its truths
about who God is, his guidelines for your life, and how
he wants to do his work on earth through you.

2 KINGS 6:17 | *Elisha prayed, "O LORD, open his eyes and let
him see!" The LORD opened the young man's eyes, and when
he looked up, he saw that the hillside around Elisha was filled
with horses and chariots of fire.*

JOHN 20:27-29 | *[Jesus] said to Thomas, "Put your finger here,
and look at my hands. Put your hand into the wound in my side.*

*Don't be faithless any longer. Believe!" "My Lord and my God!"
Thomas exclaimed. Then Jesus told him, "You believe because you
have seen me. Blessed are those who believe without seeing me."*

The strongest faith is one based not on the physical senses
but on spiritual conviction. There is a spiritual element to
this world that we cannot see, but which is very real. Your
faith will become stronger the more you allow the Holy
Spirit to strengthen your "spiritual vision" so that you can
sense and see the results of God working in your life and in
the lives of those around you.

Promise from God ACTS 16:31 | *Believe in the Lord Jesus
and you will be saved.*

FINISHING

Why is it important to finish what I begin?

ECCLESIASTES 5:5 | *It is better to say nothing than to make
a promise and not keep it.*

LUKE 14:28-30 | *Don't begin until you count the cost. . . .
Otherwise, you might complete only the foundation before
running out of money, and then everyone would laugh at you.
They would say, "There's the person who started that building
and couldn't afford to finish it!"*

If you don't finish what you promised to do, you hurt your
reputation.

ECCLESIASTES 7:8 | *Finishing is better than starting. Patience
is better than pride.*

Following through helps you develop patience and humility in your character.

JOHN 4:34 | *Jesus explained: "My nourishment comes from doing the will of God, who sent me, and from finishing his work."*

JOHN 17:1, 4 | *Jesus looked up to heaven and said, "Father, . . . I brought glory to you here on earth by completing the work you gave me to do."*

When you finish the task God has given you to do, you will experience blessing and God will receive glory.

1 CORINTHIANS 9:24 | *Don't you realize that in a race everyone runs, but only one person gets the prize? So run to win!*

You won't receive your reward if you don't finish.

Are some things better left unfinished?

1 CHRONICLES 27:24 | *Joab son of Zeruiah began the census but never finished it because the anger of God fell on Israel. The total number was never recorded in King David's official records.*

If it becomes clear that what you are doing is against God's will, then leave it unfinished.

GENESIS 11:8 | *The LORD scattered them all over the world, and they stopped building the city.*

Don't finish something you never should have started!

Promise from God PHILIPPIANS 1:6 | *I am certain that God, who began the good work within you, will continue his work until it is finally finished on the day when Christ Jesus returns.*

FORGIVENESS

Do I have to forgive others who hurt me?

MATTHEW 6:14-15 | *If you forgive those who sin against you, your heavenly Father will forgive you. But if you refuse to forgive others, your Father will not forgive your sins.*

You will receive God's forgiveness when you are willing to forgive others who have wronged you. Being unwilling to forgive shows that you have not understood or benefited from God's forgiveness.

MATTHEW 18:21-22 | *Peter came to him and asked, "Lord, how often should I forgive someone who sins against me? Seven times?" "No, not seven times," Jesus replied, "but seventy times seven!"*

LUKE 17:3-4 | *If another believer sins, rebuke that person; then if there is repentance, forgive. Even if that person wrongs you seven times a day and each time turns again and asks forgiveness, you must forgive.*

Just as God forgives you without limit, you should forgive others without counting how many times you do it. God commands you to forgive, even if you must do it over and over again.

LUKE 23:34 | *Jesus said, "Father, forgive them, for they don't know what they are doing."*

Jesus forgave those who mocked him and killed him. He expects us to follow his example.

COLOSSIANS 3:13 | *Make allowance for each other's faults, and forgive anyone who offends you. Remember, the Lord forgave you, so you must forgive others.*

1 PETER 3:9 | *Don't repay evil for evil. Don't retaliate with insults when people insult you. Instead, pay them back with a blessing. That is what God has called you to do, and he will bless you for it.*

When people say hurtful things about you, God wants you to respond by blessing them, in an attitude of forgiveness.

I've done some pretty awful things. How can God forgive me?

PSALM 51:4 | *Against you, and you alone, have I sinned; I have done what is evil in your sight.*

Realize that ultimately God is the one who has been wronged by your sin, so he is the first one you need to ask for forgiveness.

2 CHRONICLES 7:14 | *If my people who are called by my name will humble themselves and pray and seek my face and turn from their wicked ways, I will hear from heaven and will forgive their sins and restore their land.*

1 JOHN 1:8-9 | *If we claim we have no sin, we are only fooling ourselves and not living in the truth. But if we confess our sins to him, he is faithful and just to forgive us our sins and to cleanse us from all wickedness.*

You will receive God's forgiveness when you confess your sins to him, stop doing what is wrong, and turn to him wholeheartedly.

MATTHEW 26:28 | *[Jesus said,] "This is my blood, which confirms the covenant between God and his people. It is poured out as a sacrifice to forgive the sins of many."*

Jesus died so that God's forgiveness would be freely available to you.

ACTS 13:38 | *We are here to proclaim that through this man Jesus there is forgiveness for your sins.*

You receive God's forgiveness first by trusting Jesus with your life and then by confessing your sins to him.

Promise from God ISAIAH 43:25 | *I—yes, I alone—will blot out your sins for my own sake and will never think of them again.*

FRIENDSHIP

What are marks of true friendship?

1 SAMUEL 18:3 | *Jonathan made a solemn pact with David, because he loved him as he loved himself.*

PROVERBS 17:17 | *A friend is always loyal, and a brother is born to help in time of need.*

True friendships are bonded by loyalty and commitment. They remain intact despite changing external circumstances.

What gets in the way of friendship?

1 SAMUEL 18:9-11 | *From that time on Saul kept a jealous eye on David. The very next day . . . Saul had a spear in his hand, and he suddenly hurled it at David, intending to pin him to the wall.*

Jealousy is a great dividing force in friendships. Envy over what your friend has soon turns to anger and bitterness, causing you to separate yourself from the one you truly cared for.

PSALM 41:9 | *Even my best friend, the one I trusted completely, . . . has turned against me.*

When trust is seriously damaged, even the closest friendship is at risk.

2 SAMUEL 13:11 | *As she was feeding him, he grabbed her and demanded, "Come to bed with me, my darling sister."*

Friendships are destroyed when boundaries are violated.

What can I do when I feel as though I don't have any friends?

JOB 19:19 | *My close friends detest me. Those I loved have turned against me.*

JOHN 5:6-7 | *[Jesus] asked him, "Would you like to get well?" "I can't, sir," the sick man said, "for I have no one to put me into the pool when the water bubbles up. Someone else always gets there ahead of me."*

Everyone goes through times when it seems as if their friends have deserted them. Examine your relationships to make sure you are not the one causing a breach.

MATTHEW 7:12 | *Do to others whatever you would like them to do to you.*

Everyone wants to have good friends, but few are willing to invest the time and effort necessary to build such relationships. Even if you don't make friends quickly and easily, you can build strong, lasting friendships over time.

It might help you to consider the qualities you desire in a good friend, and then work to develop those qualities in your own life.

JOHN 15:15 | *[Jesus said,] "I no longer call you slaves. . . . Now you are my friends."*

HEBREWS 13:5 | *God has said, "I will never fail you. I will never abandon you."*

Remember that God is your constant friend; he will never leave you. And there's an added bonus: Keep showing God's love to others, and they will be drawn to you.

EPHESIANS 4:32 | *Be kind to each other, tenderhearted, forgiving one another, just as God through Christ has forgiven you.*

Acts of kindness and generosity will attract others to you.

Promise from God ROMANS 5:11 | *Our Lord Jesus Christ has made us friends of God.*

GAMBLING

Why do people gamble?

LUKE 12:15 | *Beware! Guard against every kind of greed. Life is not measured by how much you own.*

Gambling is often motivated by greed—by always wanting more because people are not satisfied with what they have.

PROVERBS 13:4 | *Lazy people want much but get little, but those who work hard will prosper.*

PROVERBS 21:25-26 | *Despite their desires, the lazy will come to ruin, for their hands refuse to work. Some people are always greedy for more, but the godly love to give!*

Gambling is often a form of laziness because it appears to be an easier way to get a large amount of money than working for it.

JUDGES 14:12-13 | *Samson said to them, "Let me tell you a riddle. If you solve my riddle during these seven days of the celebration, I will give you thirty fine linen robes and thirty sets of festive clothing. But if you can't solve it, then you must give me thirty fine linen robes and thirty sets of festive clothing." "All right," they agreed, "let's hear your riddle."*

People often gamble for the thrill of the moment, to experience a high from winning or besting an opponent.

Why should I stay away from gambling?

PROVERBS 1:19 | *Such is the fate of all who are greedy for money; it robs them of life.*

PROVERBS 28:22 | *Greedy people try to get rich quick but don't realize they're headed for poverty.*

Gambling is motivated by the hope of getting rich quick, but the Bible warns you to stay away from it because it often ends in poverty.

1 THESSALONIANS 4:11-12 | *Make it your goal to live a quiet life, minding your own business and working with your hands, just as we instructed you before. Then people who are not Christians will respect the way you live, and you will not need to depend on others.*

God values those who work to support themselves and warns against get-rich-quick schemes.

Promise from God EPHESIANS 5:5 | *You can be sure that no immoral, impure, or greedy person will inherit the Kingdom of Christ and of God. For a greedy person is an idolater, worshiping the things of this world.*

GENEROSITY

What is generosity?

DEUTERONOMY 15:7-8 | *If there are any poor Israelites in your towns when you arrive in the land the LORD your God is giving you, do not be hard-hearted or tightfisted toward them. Instead, be generous and lend them whatever they need.*

DEUTERONOMY 16:17 | *All must give as they are able, according to the blessings given to them by the LORD your God.*

HEBREWS 13:16 | *Don't forget to do good and to share with those in need. These are the sacrifices that please God.*

Generosity involves sharing with others out of the blessings you have received from God.

2 CORINTHIANS 8:3 | *I can testify that they gave not only what they could afford, but far more. And they did it of their own free will.*

2 CORINTHIANS 9:7 | *You must each decide in your heart how much to give. And don't give reluctantly or in response to pressure. "For God loves a person who gives cheerfully."*

Generosity is not just about what you give but the attitude with which you give it.

In what ways has God been generous with me?

ROMANS 5:15 | *There is a great difference between Adam's sin and God's gracious gift. For the sin of this one man, Adam, brought death to many. But even greater is God's wonderful grace and his gift of forgiveness to many through this other man, Jesus Christ.*

ROMANS 10:12 | *[The Lord] gives generously to all who call on him.*

God has generously given you forgiveness and the gift of eternal life in heaven.

TITUS 3:6 | *He generously poured out the Spirit upon us through Jesus Christ our Savior.*

God has generously given you the Holy Spirit through Christ.

Promise from God PROVERBS 11:25 | *The generous will prosper; those who refresh others will themselves be refreshed.*

GOALS

Why are goals important?

GENESIS 12:1-2 | *The LORD had said to Abram, "Leave your native country, your relatives, and your father's family, and go to the land that I will show you. I will make you into a great nation. I will bless you and make you famous, and you will be a blessing to others."*

God's goals for you should set the agenda for your life. His promise to Abram gave Abram such a strong sense of purpose and direction that he risked everything to pursue it.

MARK 10:45 | *Even the Son of Man came not to be served but to serve others and to give his life as a ransom for many.*

Goals keep you focused on your primary mission. No matter what was going on around him, Jesus never lost sight of the reason he came to earth.

JOB 6:11 | *I don't have the strength to endure. I have nothing to live for.*

Goals give you strength and endurance and purpose.

PSALM 40:8 | *I take joy in doing your will, my God, for your instructions are written on my heart.*

Good goals bring joy.

PROVERBS 4:25-27 | *Look straight ahead, and fix your eyes on what lies before you. Mark out a straight path for your feet; stay on the safe path. Don't get sidetracked; keep your feet from following evil.*

Goals help you keep your eyes on what you are pursuing so you don't turn away toward temptation.

What kinds of goals does God want me to have?

ISAIAH 26:8 | *LORD, we show our trust in you by obeying your laws; our heart's desire is to glorify your name.*

JEREMIAH 45:5 | *Are you seeking great things for yourself? Don't do it!*

You should pursue goals that bring glory to God, not to yourself.

ROMANS 14:19 | *Let us aim for harmony in the church and try to build each other up.*

1 CORINTHIANS 14:1 | *Let love be your highest goal!*

You should make it a goal to foster harmony and love with other Christians.

2 CORINTHIANS 5:9 | *Our goal is to please him.*

Whatever you do, your primary goal should be to please God.

Promise from God PSALM 37:4 | *Take delight in the LORD, and he will give you your heart's desires.*

GOD'S WILL

Does God really have a plan for my life?

PHILIPPIANS 1:6 | *I am certain that God, who began the good work within you, will continue his work until it is finally finished on the day when Christ Jesus returns.*

God has both a general plan and a specific plan for your life. He wants you to follow a certain path to fulfill his purpose for you, and he cares about the details along the way.

JEREMIAH 29:11 | *"I know the plans I have for you," says the LORD. "They are plans for good and not for disaster, to give you a future and a hope."*

God's plans for you are always for your good. The unknown can be frightening, but when you belong to God, you can rest in the knowledge that he has good things planned for your future.

PSALM 138:8 | *The LORD will work out his plans for my life.*

God has a plan for your life, but it is not an automated script you must follow. It is a journey with various important destinations and appointments, and there is a great deal of freedom as to the pace and scope of the travel. God's plan for you will always have a sense of mystery, but you can be certain that he will guide you as long as you rely on his leading.

What can I do to discover God's will for my life?

ISAIAH 2:3 | *Come, let us go up to the mountain of the LORD, to the house of Jacob's God. There he will teach us his ways, and we will walk in his paths.*

You can't sit around waiting for God to reveal his will for you; you must actively look for it. Give yourself completely to knowing God's will. Seek it passionately. You seek God's will by praying, reading the Bible, conversing with mature believers and reliable advisers, and examining the circumstances you face.

JAMES 1:5 | *If you need wisdom, ask our generous God, and he will give it to you. He will not rebuke you for asking.*

Pray, asking God to reveal his will to you.

ACTS 21:14 | *When it was clear that we couldn't persuade him, we gave up and said, "The LORD's will be done."*

Sometimes God's will for you becomes evident through circumstances beyond your control. Allow God to work out his will in the way he knows is best. You will discover that you like where he takes you.

What are some things that I can know are God's will for me?

EXODUS 20:1 | *God gave the people all these instructions: . . .*

God's will is that you obey his laws for living.

PROVERBS 16:3 | *Commit your actions to the LORD, and your plans will succeed.*

God's will is that you do everything as doing it for him and under his control. God may not have revealed all of his plan for you now, but he has revealed everything you need to know to live for him today.

1 CORINTHIANS 14:1 | *Let love be your highest goal!*

God's will for you today is that you love others.

MARK 10:45 | *Even the Son of Man came not to be served but to serve others and to give his life as a ransom for many.*

God's will for you today is that you serve others, putting their needs above your own.

Promise from God PROVERBS 3:6 | *Seek his will in all you do, and he will show you which path to take.*

HABITS

How can I deal with bad habits?

ROMANS 7:15 | *I don't really understand myself, for I want to do what is right, but I don't do it. Instead, I do what I hate.*

One of the best ways to deal with bad habits is to recognize them for what they are and confess them honestly. Paul knew that he could not kick the habit of sin completely. You may have to break a habit gradually, one step at a time.

1 JOHN 2:15 | *Do not love this world nor the things it offers you.*

Sin often appears lovely and attractive. Breaking a bad habit can be hard if you are giving up something you enjoy. Understand that there may be a sense of loss. But losing a bad habit ultimately brings the deeper satisfaction of doing what is pleasing to God.

COLOSSIANS 3:2 | *Think about the things of heaven, not the things of earth.*

It is much easier to break bad habits if you replace them with good habits.

How can I develop good habits?

HEBREWS 10:25 | *Let us not neglect our meeting together, as some people do.*

Regularly meeting together with other believers provides necessary fellowship, it encourages group Bible study, it keeps you busy when you might otherwise slip into bad habits, and it offers an accountability group.

GENESIS 26:21-22 | *Isaac's men then dug another well, but again there was a dispute over it. . . . Abandoning that one, Isaac moved on and dug another well. This time there was no dispute over it.*

Stay away from the source of your bad habit. Isaac pursued a habit of living in peace by staying away from the source of conflict, the Philistines, even at great cost.

PSALM 28:7 | *The LORD is my strength and shield. I trust him with all my heart. He helps me, and my heart is filled with joy. I burst out in songs of thanksgiving.*

As a young boy, David developed the habit of talking to God, singing songs about him, and writing psalms. This laid a foundation for trusting and following God all his life.

How can I pass on good habits to my children?

DEUTERONOMY 11:19 | *Teach [God's words] to your children. Talk about them when you are at home and when you are on the road, when you are going to bed and when you are getting up.*

1 TIMOTHY 4:12 | *Be an example to all believers in what you say, in the way you live, in your love, your faith, and your purity.*

Children most often learn by example. Be purposeful about modeling good habits for your children. Tell them why you follow God and how you have seen him work in your life. Make it a habit to pass on a godly heritage.

Promise from God ROMANS 8:6 | *Letting your sinful nature control your mind leads to death. But letting the Spirit control your mind leads to life and peace.*

HELP

In what ways does God help me?

DEUTERONOMY 33:29 | *Who else is like you, a people saved by the LORD? He is your protecting shield and your triumphant sword!*

PSALM 28:7 | *The LORD is my strength and shield. I trust him with all my heart. He helps me, and my heart is filled with joy. I burst out in songs of thanksgiving.*

God helps you by giving you strength to face any crisis. God protects you from being defeated by the enemy and gives you spiritual victory.

ISAIAH 30:21 | *Your own ears will hear [the Lord]. Right behind you a voice will say, "This is the way you should go," whether to the right or to the left.*

God, through his Holy Spirit, helps you by giving you an extra measure of wisdom and discernment.

ROMANS 8:26 | *We don't know what God wants us to pray for. But the Holy Spirit prays for us with groanings that cannot be expressed in words.*

God helps you to pray when you don't know what to say.

GENESIS 2:18 | *The LORD God said, "It is not good for the man to be alone. I will make a helper who is just right for him."*

God helps you by giving you other people to love and support you.

In what ways can I help others?

ACTS 16:9 | *Paul had a vision: A man from Macedonia in northern Greece was standing there, pleading with him, "Come over to Macedonia and help us!"*

You can tell others the Good News of Jesus, giving them an opportunity to experience salvation and eternal life.

ROMANS 12:13 | *When God's people are in need, be ready to help them. Always be eager to practice hospitality.*

You should do whatever you can to help those in need, even if it involves hardship or risk for you. And you can help others by showing hospitality.

GALATIANS 6:1 | *If another believer is overcome by some sin, you who are godly should gently and humbly help that person back onto the right path.*

You can help other believers who have stumbled in their walk with God, showing them how to restore their relationship with him.

Promise from God HEBREWS 13:6 | *The LORD is my helper, so I will have no fear. What can mere people do to me?*

HOLINESS

What does it mean to be holy?

2 CORINTHIANS 6:17 | *Come out from among unbelievers, and separate yourselves from them, says the LORD.*

2 CORINTHIANS 7:1 | *Let us cleanse ourselves from everything that can defile our body or spirit. And let us work toward complete holiness because we fear God.*

Holiness is more than the absence of sin; it is the practice of righteousness, purity, and godliness. Holiness means to be wholly dedicated and devoted to God, to be distinct and separate from the world's way of living, and to be committed to right living and purity.

1 THESSALONIANS 4:3, 7 | *God's will is for you to be holy, so stay away from all sexual sin. . . . God has called us to live holy lives, not impure lives.*

Sexual purity is a necessary prerequisite for holiness.

In what ways is God holy?

1 SAMUEL 6:20 | *"Who is able to stand in the presence of the LORD, this holy God?" they cried out.*

God is completely separate from sin and evil. He is perfect and has no sin in him.

ISAIAH 6:3 | *Holy, holy, holy is the LORD of Heaven's Armies! The whole earth is filled with his glory!*

God is dazzling and glorious in his absolute purity.

AMOS 4:2 | *The Sovereign LORD has sworn this by his holiness.*

When God makes a promise, his holiness ensures that he will do what he says.

HEBREWS 7:26 | *He is the kind of high priest we need because he is holy and blameless, unstained by sin. He has been set apart from sinners and has been given the highest place of honor in heaven.*

Christ is completely holy because he is completely free from sin.

MATTHEW 13:41 | *The Son of Man will send his angels, and they will remove from his Kingdom everything that causes sin and all who do evil.*

God's holiness will not tolerate evil in his eternal Kingdom.

How is it possible for me to be holy?

JOB 14:4 | *Who can bring purity out of an impure person? No one!*

You cannot create holiness in yourself because you were born with a sinful nature.

LEVITICUS 21:8 | *I, the LORD, am holy, and I make you holy.*

God is the only one who can make you holy.

DEUTERONOMY 14:2 | *You have been set apart as holy to the LORD your God, and he has chosen you from all the nations of the earth to be his own special treasure.*

God makes you holy by setting you apart to himself.

COLOSSIANS 1:22 | *Now he has reconciled you to himself through the death of Christ in his physical body. As a result, he has brought you into his own presence, and you are holy and blameless as you stand before him without a single fault.*

Through Christ's death, you can stand holy and blameless in God's presence.

JOHN 17:1, 17 | *Jesus looked up to heaven and said, "Father, . . . make them holy by your truth; teach them your word, which is truth."*

You develop holiness as you learn God's truth from his Word.

Promise from God 1 THESSALONIANS 3:13 | *May he . . . make your hearts strong, blameless, and holy as you stand before God our Father when our Lord Jesus comes again with all his holy people.*

HONESTY

Why is honesty so important?

PSALM 24:3-4 | *Who may climb the mountain of the LORD? Who may stand in his holy place? Only those whose hands and hearts are pure, who . . . never tell lies.*

If you want to approach God, you must be honest, practicing purity, integrity, and a desire to do what is right.

PROVERBS 16:11 | *The LORD demands accurate scales and balances; he sets the standards for fairness.*

God is honest and expects you to be honest as well.

PROVERBS 12:5 | *The plans of the godly are just.*

MATTHEW 12:33 | *A tree is identified by its fruit. If a tree is good, its fruit will be good. If a tree is bad, its fruit will be bad.*

LUKE 16:10 | *If you are dishonest in little things, you won't be honest with greater responsibilities.*

Your level of honesty demonstrates the quality of your character.

1 TIMOTHY 1:19 | *Cling to your faith in Christ, and keep your conscience clear. For some people have deliberately violated their consciences; as a result, their faith has been shipwrecked.*

Honesty brings a clear conscience.

DEUTERONOMY 25:13-15 | *You must use accurate scales when you weigh out merchandise, and you must use full and honest measures. Yes, always use honest weights and measures, so that you may enjoy a long life in the land the LORD your God is giving you.*

Honesty brings blessings from God.

Promise from God PSALM 37:37 | *Look at those who are honest and good, for a wonderful future awaits those who love peace.*

HOPE

Where do I find hope?

PSALM 39:7 | *Lord, where do I put my hope? My only hope is in you.*

The Lord himself is the source of hope because he holds the future in his hands.

Why should I trust God as my hope?

HEBREWS 6:18-19 | *God has given both his promise and his oath. These two things are unchangeable because it is impossible for God to lie. Therefore, we who have fled to him for refuge can have great confidence as we hold to the hope that lies before us. This hope is a strong and trustworthy anchor for our souls. It leads us through the curtain into God's inner sanctuary.*

HEBREWS 10:23 | *Let us hold tightly without wavering to the hope we affirm, for God can be trusted to keep his promise.*

1 PETER 1:21 | *Through Christ you have come to trust in God. And you have placed your faith and hope in God because he raised Christ from the dead and gave him great glory.*

God cannot lie because he is truth. God, therefore, cannot break his promises. His Word stands forever. You can trust

God as your hope because he alone conquered death by raising Christ from the dead.

Where can I go to reinforce my hope?

PSALM 119:43, 74, 81, 114, 147 | *Do not snatch your word of truth from me, for your regulations are my only hope. . . . May all who fear you find in me a cause for joy, for I have put my hope in your word. . . . I am worn out waiting for your rescue, but I have put my hope in your word. . . . You are my refuge and my shield; your word is my source of hope. . . . I rise early, before the sun is up; I cry out for help and put my hope in your words.*

ROMANS 15:4 | *Such things were written in the Scriptures long ago to teach us. And the Scriptures give us hope and encouragement as we wait patiently for God's promises to be fulfilled.*

Each day you can study God's Word to have your hope renewed and reinforced. His Word never fails or wavers.

Promise from God JEREMIAH 29:11 | *"I know the plans I have for you," says the LORD. "They are plans for good and not for disaster, to give you a future and a hope."*

HUMILITY

What is true humility?

ZEPHANIAH 3:12 | *Those who are left will be the lowly and humble, for it is they who trust in the name of the LORD.*

Being humble is not thinking too highly of yourself.

MATTHEW 18:4 | *Anyone who becomes as humble as this little child is the greatest in the Kingdom of Heaven.*

Being humble is being childlike. It is an attitude of total trust in God.

TITUS 3:2 | *They must not slander anyone and must avoid quarreling. Instead, they should be gentle and show true humility to everyone.*

Being humble is being gentle and amicable to all.

PSALM 51:3-4 | *I recognize my rebellion; it haunts me day and night. Against you, and you alone, have I sinned; I have done what is evil in your sight. You will be proved right in what you say, and your judgment against me is just.*

Being humble is being willing to admit and confess sin.

PROVERBS 12:23 | *The wise don't make a show of their knowledge, but fools broadcast their foolishness.*

Being humble is refraining from drawing attention to yourself, even for those areas in which you are gifted.

PROVERBS 13:10 | *Pride leads to conflict; those who take advice are wise.*

Being humble allows you to seek advice.

GENESIS 32:9-10 | *Jacob prayed, "O God . . . you promised me, 'I will treat you kindly.' I am not worthy of all the unfailing love and faithfulness you have shown to me, your servant."*

Being humble is recognizing how much you need God and how much he provides for you!

How do I become humble?

DEUTERONOMY 8:2-3 | *Remember how the LORD your God led you through the wilderness for these forty years. . . . He humbled you by letting you go hungry and then feeding you with manna. . . . He did it to teach you that people do not live by bread alone; rather, we live by every word that comes from the mouth of the LORD.*

Humility comes when you recognize that you need God and then watch him meet your needs.

How does God respond to a humble spirit?

PSALM 138:6 | *Though the LORD is great, he cares for the humble, but he keeps his distance from the proud.*

God takes care of the humble.

ISAIAH 29:19 | *The humble will be filled with fresh joy from the LORD. The poor will rejoice in the Holy One of Israel.*

God gives joy to the humble.

MATTHEW 18:4 | *Anyone who becomes as humble as this little child is the greatest in the Kingdom of Heaven.*

God honors and blesses the humble.

Promise from God MATTHEW 23:12 | *Those who exalt themselves will be humbled, and those who humble themselves will be exalted.*

HYPOCRISY

What does God think about hypocrisy?

PSALM 50:16-17 | *Why bother reciting my decrees and pretending to obey my covenant? For you refuse my discipline and treat my words like trash.*

God is angry when people pretend to be good.

AMOS 5:21 | *I hate all your show and pretense—the hypocrisy of your religious festivals and solemn assemblies.*

God hates religious hypocrisy.

ISAIAH 29:13 | *The LORD says, "These people say they are mine. They honor me with their lips, but their hearts are far from me. And their worship of me is nothing but man-made rules learned by rote."*

God sees through people's hypocrisy; he is not fooled.

How should I respond when others are hypocritical?

PSALM 26:4 | *I do not spend time with liars or go along with hypocrites.*

Don't spend lots of time with hypocritical people because it is easy to pick up their habits.

GALATIANS 2:11 | *When Peter came to Antioch, I had to oppose him to his face, for what he did was very wrong.*

When a brother or sister in Christ is acting hypocritically, sometimes confrontation is necessary.

How do I avoid being a hypocrite?

MATTHEW 5:23-24 | *If you are presenting a sacrifice at the altar in the Temple and you suddenly remember that someone has something against you, leave your sacrifice there at the altar. Go and be reconciled to that person. Then come and offer your sacrifice to God.*

Take care of any wrong in your private life before worshiping God publicly.

JAMES 4:8 | *Come close to God, and God will come close to you. Wash your hands, you sinners; purify your hearts, for your loyalty is divided between God and the world.*

Following God sincerely will help you get rid of hypocrisy in your life.

Promise from God HEBREWS 10:22 | *Let us go right into the presence of God with sincere hearts fully trusting him. For our guilty consciences have been sprinkled with Christ's blood to make us clean, and our bodies have been washed with pure water.*

IDOLATRY

What is idolatry?

EXODUS 20:1-5 | *God gave the people all these instructions: "I am the LORD your God, who rescued you from the land of Egypt, the place of your slavery. You must not have any other god but me. You must not make for yourself an idol of any kind or an image of anything in the heavens or on the earth or in the sea.*

You must not bow down to them or worship them, for I, the LORD your God, am a jealous God who will not tolerate your affection for any other gods."

Idolatry is worshiping anything or anyone other than God himself.

LUKE 12:34 | *Wherever your treasure is, there the desires of your heart will also be.*

1 JOHN 5:21 | *Keep away from anything that might take God's place in your hearts.*

Idolatry is allowing anything else to become more important than God. Whatever you attach supreme value to—whether it is a person, possession, money, power, or education—becomes a god that controls your life.

What kinds of idols do people worship today?

LEVITICUS 19:4 | *Do not put your trust in idols or make metal images of gods for yourselves. I am the LORD your God.*

People in our culture don't often make statues to worship, but many people do worship man-made objects.

DEUTERONOMY 4:15-18 | *Be very careful! You did not see the LORD's form on the day he spoke to you from the heart of the fire at Mount Sinai. So do not corrupt yourselves by making an idol in any form—whether of a man or a woman, an animal on the ground, a bird in the sky, a small animal that scurries along the ground, or a fish in the deepest sea.*

Some people worship images, not knowing that this is idolatry.

DEUTERONOMY 4:19 | *When you look up into the sky and see the sun, moon, and stars—all the forces of heaven—don't be seduced into worshiping them. The LORD your God gave them to all the peoples of the earth.*

ROMANS 1:21, 23, 25 | *Yes, they knew God, but they wouldn't worship him as God or even give him thanks. . . . And instead of worshiping the glorious, ever-living God, . . . they worshiped and served the things God created instead of the Creator himself, who is worthy of eternal praise!*

Many people worship Creation rather than the Creator, God himself.

2 CHRONICLES 33:6 | *Manasseh . . . practiced sorcery, divination, and witchcraft, and he consulted with mediums and psychics. He did much that was evil in the LORD's sight, arousing his anger.*

Some people worship spiritual powers that are not from God.

ACTS 10:25-26 | *As Peter entered his home, Cornelius fell at his feet and worshiped him. But Peter pulled him up and said, "Stand up! I'm a human being just like you!"*

Many people make the mistake of worshiping celebrities and other popular figures.

Promise from God EZEKIEL 36:25 | *I will sprinkle clean water on you, and you will be clean. Your filth will be washed away, and you will no longer worship idols.*

INTIMACY

How can I experience true and lasting intimacy in my marriage?

PROVERBS 5:15, 19 | *Drink water from your own well—share your love only with your wife. . . . May you always be captivated by her love.*

PROVERBS 18:22 | *The man who finds a wife finds a treasure.*

1 CORINTHIANS 7:3 | *The husband should fulfill his wife's sexual needs, and the wife should fulfill her husband's needs.*

EPHESIANS 5:21, 25 | *Submit to one another out of reverence for Christ. . . . Husbands, . . . love your wives, just as Christ loved the church. He gave up his life for her.*

True and lasting intimacy for marriage partners is based upon the following: faithfulness, rejoicing in each other, satisfying each other emotionally and sexually, living happily with each other, talking together about the Lord and spiritual things, giving thanks to the Lord together, and submitting to each other. For husbands, it means accepting your wife as a blessing from the Lord, recognizing the great value of your wife, recognizing that your wife can truly bring you delight and satisfaction, and loving your wife as passionately as Christ loved the church.

How can I experience an intimate relationship with God?

GENESIS 5:23-24 | *Enoch lived 365 years, walking in close fellowship with God. Then one day he disappeared, because God took him.*

Walk closely with God—daily and consistently.

GENESIS 6:9 | *This is the account of Noah and his family. Noah was a righteous man, the only blameless person living on earth at the time, and he walked in close fellowship with God.*

Live the way God wants you to live—daily and consistently.

PSALM 27:8 | *My heart has heard you say, "Come and talk with me." And my heart responds, "LORD, I am coming."*

PSALM 145:18 | *The LORD is close to all who call on him, yes, to all who call on him in truth.*

Talk with God—daily and consistently.

JAMES 4:8 | *Come close to God, and God will come close to you. Wash your hands, you sinners; purify your hearts, for your loyalty is divided between God and the world.*

Stay close to God and purify your heart before him—daily and consistently.

EXODUS 34:14 | *You must worship no other gods, for the LORD, whose very name is Jealous, is a God who is jealous about his relationship with you.*

Worship God only—daily and consistently.

MATTHEW 22:37 | *Jesus replied, "You must love the LORD your God with all your heart, all your soul, and all your mind."*

Love God completely—daily and consistently.

ROMANS 5:11 | *Now we can rejoice in our wonderful new relationship with God because our Lord Jesus Christ has made us friends of God.*

Put your trust in Jesus Christ—daily and consistently.

Promise from God 1 CHRONICLES 28:9 | *Learn to know the God of your ancestors intimately. Worship and serve him with your whole heart and a willing mind. For the LORD sees every heart and knows every plan and thought. If you seek him, you will find him.*

JEALOUSY

Why is jealousy so dangerous?

PROVERBS 14:30 | *A peaceful heart leads to a healthy body; jealousy is like cancer in the bones.*

Jealousy eats away at you, arousing the destructive emotions of anger and bitterness rather than your being content with what you have and genuine happiness over the success of others.

PROVERBS 27:4 | *Anger is cruel, and wrath is like a flood, but jealousy is even more dangerous.*

Jealousy tears families and friends apart because it brings out a spirit of negative competition.

What can jealousy lead to?

GENESIS 4:4-5 | *The LORD accepted Abel and his gift, but he did not accept Cain and his gift. This made Cain very angry, and he looked dejected.*

Jealousy can lead to hard feelings stemming from the competition for honor and approval.

JUDGES 12:1 | *The people of Ephraim mobilized an army and crossed over the Jordan River to Zaphon. They sent this message to Jephthah: "Why didn't you call for us to help you fight against the Ammonites? We are going to burn down your house with you in it!"*

Jealousy turns friends into enemies.

PROVERBS 12:12 | *Thieves are jealous of each other's loot, but the godly are well rooted and bear their own fruit.*

Jealousy for what others have causes people to steal. Generous people, on the other hand, love to give.

What does it mean that God is a jealous God?

EXODUS 34:14 | *You must worship no other gods, for the LORD, whose very name is Jealous, is a God who is jealous about his relationship with you.*

DEUTERONOMY 5:9 | *I, the LORD your God, am a jealous God who will not tolerate your affection for any other gods.*

God deserves all your honor, praise, and love. He becomes jealous when people give honor, praise, and love to other things because what is due him has been squandered elsewhere.

Promise from God   PROVERBS 14:30 | *A peaceful heart leads to a healthy body; jealousy is like cancer in the bones.*

JUDGING OTHERS

What does God think when I judge others?

1 CORINTHIANS 4:5 | *Don't make judgments about anyone ahead of time—before the Lord returns. For he will bring our darkest*

secrets to light and will reveal our private motives. Then God will give to each one whatever praise is due.

Be very slow to judge others, because only God is capable of judging perfectly every time.

ROMANS 2:1 | *You may think you can condemn such people, but you are just as bad, and you have no excuse! When you say they are wicked and should be punished, you are condemning yourself, for you who judge others do these very same things.*

When you condemn others for their sin without first carefully considering your own sin, God sees your hypocrisy.

1 SAMUEL 16:7 | *The LORD said to Samuel, "Don't judge by his appearance or height, for I have rejected him. The LORD doesn't see things the way you see them. People judge by outward appearance, but the LORD looks at the heart."*

God doesn't want you to make judgments based on what you see.

LEVITICUS 19:15 | *Do not twist justice in legal matters by favoring the poor or being partial to the rich and powerful. Always judge people fairly.*

When you have to make a judgment, do so with fairness and integrity.

What are the consequences of judging others?

2 SAMUEL 12:5-7 | *David was furious. "As surely as the LORD lives," he vowed, "any man who would do such a thing deserves to die! He must repay four lambs to the poor man for the one*

he stole and for having no pity." Then Nathan said to David, "You are that man!"

If you are too quick to judge others, you may be found guilty of the same things.

MATTHEW 7:2 | *You will be treated as you treat others. The standard you use in judging is the standard by which you will be judged.*

LUKE 6:37 | *Do not condemn others, or it will all come back against you. Forgive others, and you will be forgiven.*

You will be judged by the same standard you use, so it's better to be merciful and forgiving than harsh and critical.

Promise from God MATTHEW 7:1 | *Do not judge others, and you will not be judged.*

LEADERSHIP

What are the qualities of a good leader?

GENESIS 12:1, 4 | *The LORD had said to Abram, "Leave your native country, your relatives, and your father's family, and go to the land that I will show you." . . . So Abram departed as the LORD had instructed, and Lot went with him.*

1 KINGS 22:14 | *As surely as the LORD lives, I will say only what the LORD tells me to say.*

A good leader follows the Lord's leadership.

NUMBERS 20:12 | *The LORD said to Moses and Aaron, "Because you did not trust me enough to demonstrate my holiness to the people of Israel, you will not lead them into the land I am giving them!"*

A good leader demonstrates God's character by example.

DEUTERONOMY 1:12-13 | *[Moses said,] "How can I deal with all your problems and bickering? Choose some well-respected men from each tribe who are known for their wisdom and understanding, and I will appoint them as your leaders."*

A wise leader delegates some of his responsibilities to trustworthy subordinates.

MICAH 3:1 | *Listen, you leaders of Israel! You are supposed to know right from wrong.*

Good leaders are dedicated to doing what is right.

NEHEMIAH 5:9 | *I pressed further, "What you are doing is not right!"*

A good leader courageously confronts those who are doing what is wrong.

LUKE 22:25-26 | *Jesus told them, "In this world the kings and great men lord it over their people, yet they are called 'friends of the people.' But among you it will be different. Those who are the greatest among you should take the lowest rank, and the leader should be like a servant."*

A good leader leads by serving, not by ordering others around.

How can I know if and when I should exercise leadership?

DEUTERONOMY 3:28 | *Commission Joshua and encourage and strengthen him, for he will lead the people across the Jordan. He will give them all the land you now see before you as their possession.*

If you have been commissioned to lead, then lead!

EZEKIEL 3:17 | *Son of man, I have appointed you as a watchman for Israel. Whenever you receive a message from me, warn people immediately.*

JOHN 15:16 | *You didn't choose me. I chose you. I appointed you to go and produce lasting fruit.*

You don't need to have an official position to lead, but having God's calling is essential.

Promise from God JEREMIAH 3:15 | *[The Lord says,] "I will give you shepherds after my own heart, who will guide you with knowledge and understanding."*

LISTENING

Why is listening such an important skill?

PROVERBS 1:5 | *Let the wise listen to these proverbs and become even wiser.*

Listening helps you grow and mature.

PROVERBS 5:13 | *Oh, why didn't I listen to my teachers? Why didn't I pay attention to my instructors?*

Listening helps keep you on the straight and narrow.

PROVERBS 2:1, 9 | *My child, listen to what I say. . . . Then you will understand what is right, just, and fair, and you will find the right way to go.*

Listening is essential to good decision making.

PROVERBS 8:6 | *Listen to me! For I have important things to tell you.*

Listening gives you the opportunity to hear excellent things.

EXODUS 18:24 | *Moses listened to his father-in-law's advice and followed his suggestions.*

JOB 29:21 | *Everyone listened to my advice. They were silent as they waited for me to speak.*

Listening shows that you respect others.

PROVERBS 21:13 | *Those who shut their ears to the cries of the poor will be ignored in their own time of need.*

Listening helps you connect with others.

What are some things I shouldn't listen to?

GENESIS 3:1, 6 | *[The serpent] asked the woman, "Did God really say you must not eat the fruit from any of the trees in the garden?" . . . She saw that the tree was beautiful and its fruit looked delicious. . . . So she took some of the fruit and ate it.*

MATTHEW 6:13 | *Don't let us yield to temptation, but rescue us from the evil one.*

Temptation.

MARK 13:21 | *If anyone tells you, "Look, here is the Messiah," or "There he is," don't believe it.*

2 PETER 2:1 | *There were also false prophets in Israel, just as there will be false teachers among you.*

False teaching.

PROVERBS 12:18 | *Some people make cutting remarks, but the words of the wise bring healing.*

EPHESIANS 5:4 | *Obscene stories, foolish talk, and coarse jokes—these are not for you.*

Insults, crude jokes, and off-color stories.

PROVERBS 13:5 | *The godly hate lies; the wicked cause shame and disgrace.*

Lies.

PROVERBS 29:5 | *To flatter friends is to lay a trap for their feet.*

Flattery.

How can I better listen to God?

PSALM 5:3 | *Each morning I bring my requests to you and wait expectantly.*

Come into God's presence in prayer regularly, and wait expectantly for him to speak to you.

PSALM 46:10 | *Be still, and know that I am God!*

Find times to be quiet and meditate so you will know the voice of God when he speaks.

1 KINGS 19:12 | *After the earthquake there was a fire, but the LORD was not in the fire. And after the fire there was the sound of a gentle whisper.*

Listen for God's gentle whispers, as well as his mighty shouts.

Promise from God PROVERBS 1:23 | *Come and listen to my counsel. I'll share my heart with you and make you wise.*

LOVE

Do I have to love other people? What if I don't want to?

JOHN 13:34-35 | *Love each other. Just as I have loved you, you should love each other. Your love for one another will prove to the world that you are my disciples.*

1 JOHN 2:9 | *If anyone claims, "I am living in the light," but hates a Christian brother or sister, that person is still living in darkness.*

1 JOHN 4:12 | *If we love each other, God lives in us, and his love is brought to full expression in us.*

Being a Christian comes with certain expectations, and one of them is that you will love others. Your conduct is proof of whether you love others, and loving others is proof that you belong to Christ.

What are some special gifts that come from a loving relationship?

1 CORINTHIANS 13:4-7 | *Love is patient and kind. Love is not jealous or boastful or proud or rude. It does not demand its own way. It is not irritable, and it keeps no record of being wronged. It does not rejoice about injustice but rejoices whenever the truth wins out. Love never gives up, never loses faith, is always hopeful, and endures through every circumstance.*

The gifts that come from loving relationships include forgiveness, patience, kindness, truth, justice, seeing the

best in others, loyalty at any cost, and belief in others
no matter what. Love does not allow for jealousy, pride,
contempt, selfishness, rudeness, demanding your own way,
irritability, or grudges.

Does God really love me? How can I know for sure?

ISAIAH 43:3-4 | *I am the L*ORD*, your God, the Holy One of
Israel, your Savior. . . . You are precious to me. You are
honored, and I love you.*

ROMANS 5:5 | *We know how dearly God loves us, because he has
given us the Holy Spirit to fill our hearts with his love.*

1 JOHN 4:9-10 | *God showed how much he loved us by sending
his one and only Son into the world so that we might have
eternal life through him. This is real love.*

God loves you so much that he sent his Son, Jesus, to earth
to die for you. Jesus took the punishment you deserve for
your sins. His forgiveness is so complete, it is as though
you never sinned at all. His love for you will never change
or end.

How can I show my love to God?

MATTHEW 10:42 | *If you give even a cup of cold water to one of the
least of my followers, you will surely be rewarded.*

Love God by showing love to the needy.

JOHN 14:21 | *Those who accept my commandments and obey
them are the ones who love me.*

Love God by obeying him and respecting his commandments.

JOHN 21:17 | *[Peter] said, "Lord, you know everything. You know that I love you." Jesus said, "Then feed my sheep."*

HEBREWS 6:10 | *He will not forget . . . how you have shown your love to him by caring for other believers, as you still do.*

Love God by guiding and helping other followers of Jesus and by being an example to them.

PSALM 122:1 | *I was glad when they said to me, "Let us go to the house of the LORD."*

Love God by worshiping him and praising him for who he is.

Promise from God ROMANS 8:39 | *No power in the sky above or in the earth below—indeed, nothing in all creation will ever be able to separate us from the love of God that is revealed in Christ Jesus our Lord.*

LUST

Since lust does not involve actual physical behavior, why is it wrong?

PROVERBS 4:23 | *Guard your heart above all else, for it determines the course of your life.*

LUKE 11:34 | *Your eye is a lamp that provides light for your body. When your eye is good, your whole body is filled with light. But when it is bad, your body is filled with darkness.*

Once lust is allowed to take up residence in your mind, it tends to consume your thoughts, and eventually controls your actions.

1 KINGS 11:3 | *He had 700 wives of royal birth and 300 concubines. And in fact, they did turn his heart away from the LORD.*

Because lust is a sin, dwelling in it or consistently giving in to it will negatively change your behavior and turn your heart away from God.

What is the difference between lust and love?

2 SAMUEL 13:14 | *Amnon wouldn't listen to [Tamar], and since he was stronger than she was, he raped her.*

Lust takes what it wants, regardless of the other person's needs or desires. Love gives whatever the other person needs.

1 CORINTHIANS 13:4-5 | *Love is patient and kind. . . . It does not demand its own way.*

Where love is patient and kind, lust is impatient and rude.

How can I keep my desires from becoming lustful?

MATTHEW 5:28 | *Anyone who even looks at a woman with lust has already committed adultery with her in his heart.*

You can prevent lust from taking root in your mind by avoiding a second look at temptation.

PHILIPPIANS 4:8 | *Fix your thoughts on what is true, and honorable, and right, and pure, and lovely, and admirable. Think about things that are excellent and worthy of praise.*

When you fill your heart and mind with purity and goodness, lust finds no place to dwell.

SONG OF SONGS 7:6 | *Oh, how beautiful you are! How pleasing, my love, how full of delights!*

In marriage, when you focus your desires on your wife there will be no room for lust for anyone else.

Is it possible to lust for something other than physical pleasure?

EXODUS 20:17 | *You must not covet your neighbor's house. You must not covet your neighbor's wife, male or female servant, ox or donkey, or anything else that belongs to your neighbor.*

JOB 22:24-25 | *If you give up your lust for money and throw your precious gold into the river, the Almighty himself will be your treasure.*

It is possible to lust for many things. Power, wealth, and material goods can all become objects of lust.

Promise from God   PHILIPPIANS 4:8-9 | *Fix your thoughts on what is true, and honorable, and right, and pure, and lovely, and admirable. Think about things that are excellent and worthy of praise. Keep putting into practice all you learned and received from me—everything you heard from me and saw me doing. Then the God of peace will be with you.*

MATERIALISM

Why should I avoid a lifestyle of materialism?

DEUTERONOMY 7:25 | *You must burn their idols in fire, and you must not covet the silver or gold that covers them. You must not take it or it will become a trap to you, for it is detestable to the LORD your God.*

MATTHEW 6:21 | *Wherever your treasure is, there the desires of your heart will also be.*

Materialism has great power to turn you away from God. It's not things in and of themselves; rather it's the acquiring and managing and loving of things that steal your focus from God.

GENESIS 14:12 | *They also captured Lot—Abram's nephew who lived in Sodom—and carried off everything he owned.*

Materialism makes you vulnerable to enemies who want what you have.

ECCLESIASTES 5:10 | *Those who love money will never have enough. How meaningless to think that wealth brings true happiness!*

Material things never bring the happiness they seem to promise.

MATTHEW 6:19 | *Don't store up treasures here on earth, where moths eat them and rust destroys them, and where thieves break in and steal.*

Material things are temporary. The newness wears off quickly and things break, making your efforts to acquire them a waste of time.

MARK 4:18-19 | *The seed that fell among the thorns represents others who hear God's word, but all too quickly the message is crowded out by the worries of this life, the lure of wealth, and the desire for other things, so no fruit is produced.*

Materialism makes you spiritually lazy. It is difficult to depend on Christ when you feel as though you don't need him.

How do I make sure I'm not becoming too materialistic?

JOB 1:21 | *I came naked from my mother's womb, and I will be naked when I leave. The LORD gave me what I had, and the LORD has taken it away. Praise the name of the LORD!*

Remember that everything comes from the hand of God, and everything belongs to him.

PSALM 4:7 | *You have given me greater joy than those who have abundant harvests of grain and new wine.*

Joy and satisfaction come from a relationship with God and his people; you can't have a relationship with possessions.

MATTHEW 6:20 | *Store your treasures in heaven, where moths and rust cannot destroy, and thieves do not break in and steal.*

COLOSSIANS 3:2-3 | *Think about the things of heaven, not the things of earth. For you died to this life, and your real life is hidden with Christ in God.*

Redirect your focus from material things, which don't last, to things that do—your relationships with God and with others.

LUKE 16:9 | *Use your worldly resources to benefit others and make friends. Then, when your earthly possessions are gone, they will welcome you to an eternal home.*

Focus your efforts on helping others rather than on acquiring more things for yourself. True satisfaction is found in meeting genuine needs of other people.

Promise from God 1 JOHN 2:17 | *This world is fading away, along with everything that people crave. But anyone who does what pleases God will live forever.*

MEEKNESS

Can meekness be a masculine trait?

EXODUS 32:19-20 | *When they came near the camp, Moses saw the calf and the dancing, and he burned with anger. He threw the stone tablets to the ground, smashing them at the foot of the mountain. He took the calf they had made and burned it. Then he ground it into powder, threw it into the water, and forced the people to drink it.*

NUMBERS 12:3 | *Moses was very humble—more humble than any other person on earth.*

Moses was one of the greatest and strongest leaders ever, yet he was also truly meek.

2 SAMUEL 16:9-12 | *"Why should this dead dog curse my lord the king?" Abishai son of Zeruiah demanded. "Let me go over and cut off his head!" "No!" the king said. . . . "Leave him alone and let him curse, for the LORD has told him to do it. And perhaps the LORD will see that I am being wronged and will bless me because of these curses today."*

David, the powerful warrior and king, was truly meek, as demonstrated by his response to criticism.

PROVERBS 16:32 | *Better to be patient than powerful; better to have self-control than to conquer a city.*

Patience and self-control—elements of meekness— demonstrate true inner strength.

How do I exercise meekness in my life?

PROVERBS 15:1 | *A gentle answer deflects anger, but harsh words make tempers flare.*

Answer anger with gentleness.

LUKE 6:28-29 | *Bless those who curse you. Pray for those who hurt you. If someone slaps you on one cheek, offer the other cheek also. If someone demands your coat, offer your shirt also.*

Praying for your enemies and doing good for them will help you learn meekness.

Promises from God PSALM 37:11 | *The lowly will possess the land and will live in peace and prosperity.*

MATTHEW 5:5 | *God blesses those who are humble, for they will inherit the whole earth.*

MONEY

What is the proper perspective toward money?

PSALM 23:1 | *The LORD is my shepherd; I have all that I need.*

MATTHEW 6:24 | *No one can serve two masters. . . . You cannot serve both God and money.*

The Bible mentions many wealthy people who loved God, but it says nothing negative about the *amount* of wealth they owned. Scripture doesn't focus on how much money you can or cannot have, but rather on what you do with it and your attitude toward it.

1 TIMOTHY 6:10 | *The love of money is the root of all kinds of evil.*

HEBREWS 13:5 | *Don't love money; be satisfied with what you have.*

It's not having money that's wrong; it's the love of money that can get your priorities out of line.

ISAIAH 55:2 | *Why spend your money on food that does not give you strength? . . . Listen to me, and you will eat what is good. You will enjoy the finest food.*

Too often people buy things to fill a void or a need in their lives. The Bible points to the way to acquire a deep and lasting happiness that always satisfies—finding your contentment in God.

PHILIPPIANS 4:11-12 | *I have learned how to be content with whatever I have. I know how to live on almost nothing or with everything. I have learned the secret of living in every situation, whether it is with a full stomach or empty, with plenty or little.*

PHILIPPIANS 4:19 | *This same God who takes care of me will supply all your needs from his glorious riches, which have been given to us in Christ Jesus.*

The Bible promises that God will supply all your needs. The problem comes when your definition of *need* is different from God's. When you study God's Word, you will discover what you truly need for a fulfilling life.

How can I best handle my money?

PROVERBS 3:9 | *Honor the LORD with your wealth and with the best part of everything you produce.*

MALACHI 3:10 | *"Bring all the tithes into the storehouse. . . .
If you do," says the LORD of Heaven's Armies, "I will open the
windows of heaven for you."*

Instead of viewing money as yours to use as you wish, see it
as God's to use as he wishes. Giving back to God the first
part of everything you receive will help you maintain this
perspective.

PROVERBS 21:20 | *The wise have wealth and luxury, but fools
spend whatever they get.*

PROVERBS 28:19 | *A hard worker has plenty of food, but a person
who chases fantasies ends up in poverty.*

LUKE 6:38 | *Give, and you will receive.*

2 CORINTHIANS 9:6 | *The one who plants generously will get
a generous crop.*

1 THESSALONIANS 4:11-12 | *Make it your goal to live a quiet life,
. . . working with your hands, just as we instructed you before.
Then people who are not Christians will respect the way you
live, and you will not need to depend on others.*

Properly handling money requires good stewardship in
giving, spending, and saving the money you earn. God
understands the importance of providing for the needs
of your family and preparing for the future. But he also
expects you to use your money generously to help others.

Is debt a sin?

PROVERBS 22:7 | *Just as the rich rule the poor, so the borrower
is servant to the lender.*

Although borrowing money is not in itself sinful, you must be careful and wise when you borrow so you don't become a slave to debt.

PROVERBS 6:1-3 | *If you have put up security for a friend's debt or agreed to guarantee the debt of a stranger—if you have trapped yourself by your agreement and are caught by what you said— follow my advice and save yourself, for you have placed yourself at your friend's mercy. Now swallow your pride; go and beg to have your name erased.*

Debt is not a sin, but it can be dangerous because it adds the pressure of being obligated to someone you may not even know.

ROMANS 13:8 | *Owe nothing to anyone.*

Although incurring debt may not be sinful, the failure to repay a debt is.

Promise from God MATTHEW 6:31-33 | *Don't worry about these things, saying, "What will we eat? What will we drink? What will we wear?" These things dominate the thoughts of unbelievers, but your heavenly Father already knows all your needs. Seek the Kingdom of God above all else, and live righteously, and he will give you everything you need.*

MOTIVES

As long as I do the right thing, do my motives really matter?

1 SAMUEL 16:7 | *The LORD doesn't see things the way you see them. People judge by outward appearance, but the LORD looks at the heart.*

PROVERBS 20:27 | *The LORD's light penetrates the human spirit, exposing every hidden motive.*

Your motives are very important to God. The condition of your heart is essential to the condition of your relationship with God.

What are some wrong motives?

JAMES 3:15 | *Jealousy and selfishness are not God's kind of wisdom. Such things are earthly, unspiritual, and demonic.*

1 JOHN 3:12 | *We must not be like Cain, who belonged to the evil one and killed his brother. And why did he kill him? Because Cain had been doing what was evil, and his brother had been doing what was righteous.*

If you let jealousy motivate you, your actions will be selfish and will hurt others.

GENESIS 27:11-12 | *"Look," Jacob replied to Rebekah, ". . . he'll see that I'm trying to trick him, and then he'll curse me instead of blessing me."*

Fear of getting caught is not a good enough motive because it means you're doing something wrong.

1 SAMUEL 18:17 | *Saul thought, "I'll send him out against the Philistines and let them kill him rather than doing it myself."*

If your motive is to harm someone, you are being overcome by evil desires.

What are some right motives?

2 KINGS 2:9 | *When they came to the other side, Elijah said to Elisha, "Tell me what I can do for you before I am taken away." And Elisha replied, "Please let me inherit a double share of your spirit and become your successor."*

Wanting to follow in the footsteps of a godly person is a noble motive.

2 CHRONICLES 1:10 | *[Solomon said,] "Give me the wisdom and knowledge to lead them properly, for who could possibly govern this great people of yours?"*

Solomon's motive, to serve God and rule well instead of serving himself, was pleasing to God (see verses 11-12).

JOHN 21:17 | *[Jesus] asked him, "Simon son of John, do you love me?" Peter . . . said, "Lord, you know everything. You know that I love you." Jesus said, "Then feed my sheep."*

God wants you to help people because you love Jesus, not for personal praise.

Promise from God PROVERBS 14:22 | *If you plan to do evil, you will be lost; if you plan to do good, you will receive unfailing love and faithfulness.*

OBEDIENCE

Is obedience to God really necessary if I am saved by faith?

HEBREWS 11:8 | *It was by faith that Abraham obeyed when God called him.*

Obedience is an act of faith. It shows that you trust God enough to follow his commands no matter what.

PHILIPPIANS 2:12 | *Work hard to show the results of your salvation, obeying God with deep reverence and fear.*

God's call for your obedience is based on his own commitment to your well-being. Since God is the creator of life, he knows how life is supposed to work. Obedience demonstrates your willingness to follow through on what he says is best, your desire to have a close relationship with him, and your trust that his way will work for your good.

TITUS 1:16 | *Such people claim they know God, but they deny him by the way they live. They are detestable and disobedient, worthless for doing anything good.*

If you are consistently disobedient to God, your claim that you know him is meaningless.

LEVITICUS 9:6 | *Moses said, "This is what the LORD has commanded you to do so that the glory of the LORD may appear to you."*

ACTS 5:32 | *We are witnesses of these things and so is the Holy Spirit, who is given by God to those who obey him.*

Obedience to God keeps you in fellowship with him, synchronizing you with his will.

In what ways does God want me to obey him?

DEUTERONOMY 5:32 | *You must be careful to obey all the commands of the LORD your God, following his instructions in every detail.*

True obedience is about following all God's commands to the best of your ability.

EXODUS 1:17 | *Because the midwives feared God, they refused to obey the king's orders. They allowed the boys to live, too.*

EXODUS 12:28 | *The people of Israel did just as the LORD had commanded through Moses and Aaron.*

ACTS 4:19-20 | *Peter and John replied, "Do you think God wants us to obey you rather than him? We cannot stop telling about everything we have seen and heard."*

ACTS 5:29 | *Peter and the apostles replied, "We must obey God rather than any human authority."*

ROMANS 13:1 | *Everyone must submit to governing authorities. For all authority comes from God, and those in positions of authority have been placed there by God.*

HEBREWS 13:17 | *Obey your spiritual leaders, and do what they say.*

God commands you to obey your leaders, unless they tell you to do something that contradicts God's Word.

Promise from God PSALM 119:2 | *Joyful are those who obey his laws and search for him with all their hearts.*

PARENTING

What does the Bible say about the role of parents?

2 TIMOTHY 3:15 | *You have been taught the holy Scriptures from childhood.*

Parents are to take responsibility for teaching their children to love the Word of God.

PROVERBS 3:12 | *The LORD corrects those he loves, just as a father corrects a child in whom he delights.*

HEBREWS 12:11 | *No discipline is enjoyable while it is happening— it's painful! But afterward there will be a peaceful harvest of right living for those who are trained in this way.*

Parents are to discipline their children with consistency, wisdom, and love.

GENESIS 25:28 | *Isaac loved Esau . . . , but Rebekah loved Jacob.*

Parents are not to show favoritism between children.

1 SAMUEL 2:29 | *Why do you give your sons more honor than you give me . . . !*

Parents do their children a favor when they sincerely seek what God wants—not necessarily what they want—for their children. Indulgent parents do not help their children develop character.

LUKE 15:20 | *Filled with love and compassion, he ran to his son, embraced him, and kissed him.*

The mark of a loving parent is the willingness to forgive.

How should children relate to their parents?

EXODUS 20:12 | *Honor your father and mother. Then you will live a long, full life in the land the LORD your God is giving you.*

EPHESIANS 6:1 | *Children, obey your parents because you belong to the Lord, for this is the right thing to do.*

Children have a responsibility to honor and respect their parents.

What if I am a single parent or grew up in a single-parent home?

PSALM 68:5 | *Father to the fatherless, defender of widows—this is God, whose dwelling is holy.*

God has a special place in his heart for those who are lonely or abandoned.

Promise from God PROVERBS 22:6 | *Direct your children onto the right path, and when they are older, they will not leave it.*

PATIENCE

How can I develop patience?

EXODUS 5:22 | *Moses went back to the LORD and protested, ". . . Why did you send me?"*

Focusing less on your own agenda and more on God's agenda for you will provide a big-picture perspective and help you be more patient.

PSALM 40:1 | *I waited patiently for the LORD to help me, and he turned to me and heard my cry.*

Prayer is a necessary tool for developing patience and giving you God's perspective on your situation.

HABAKKUK 2:3 | *If it seems slow in coming, wait patiently, for it will surely take place. It will not be delayed.*

God is going to do what is best for you, but his plan for you will be accomplished on his schedule, not yours. Keeping that in mind, you can actually be excited about waiting for him to act as you anticipate the good things he will work in your life.

GALATIANS 5:22 | *The Holy Spirit produces this kind of fruit in our lives: love, joy, peace, patience.*

The more you let the Holy Spirit fill and inspire you, the more patient you will become. All fruit takes time to grow and mature, including the fruit of the Holy Spirit.

ROMANS 8:25 | *If we look forward to something we don't yet have, we must wait patiently and confidently.*

ROMANS 12:12 | *Rejoice in our confident hope. Be patient in trouble, and keep on praying.*

God uses life's circumstances to develop your patience. You can't always choose the circumstances that come your way, but you can choose to learn and grow from them.

Promise from God ISAIAH 30:18 | *The LORD is a faithful God. Blessed are those who wait for his help.*

PERSISTENCE

━━━━━━━━━━━━━━━━━━━━━━━━━━━━━━━━━━━━•◄●

Why is persistence an important quality?

GENESIS 18:32 | *Abraham said, "LORD, please don't be angry with me if I speak one more time. Suppose only ten are found there?" And the LORD replied, "Then I will not destroy it for the sake of the ten."*

Persistence in prayer is vital for effective intercession.

GENESIS 32:26-29 | *The man said, "Let me go, for the dawn is breaking!" But Jacob said, "I will not let you go unless you bless me." "What is your name?" the man asked. He replied, "Jacob." "Your name will no longer be Jacob," the man told him. "From now on you will be called Israel, because you have fought with God and with men and have won." . . . Then he blessed Jacob there.*

Persistence in prayer is often the key to getting an answer from God.

LUKE 9:62 | *Jesus told him, "Anyone who puts a hand to the plow and then looks back is not fit for the Kingdom of God."*

Persistence is necessary in your walk with Christ because the Christian walk is frequently full of trials. It would be easy to give up.

How do I develop greater persistence?

1 CHRONICLES 16:11 | *Search for the LORD and for his strength; continually seek him.*

Continue steadfastly in prayer, seeking the Lord's strength for your life.

PROVERBS 4:27 | *Don't get sidetracked; keep your feet from following evil.*

GALATIANS 6:9 | *Let's not get tired of doing what is good. At just the right time we will reap a harvest of blessing if we don't give up.*

Avoid distractions that would lead you away from your goals.

EPHESIANS 6:18 | *Pray in the Spirit at all times and on every occasion. Stay alert and be persistent in your prayers for all believers everywhere.*

Rely on the power of the Holy Spirit. Persistence in prayer brings power in prayer.

HEBREWS 12:1-2 | *Let us strip off every weight that slows us down, especially the sin that so easily trips us up. And let us run with endurance the race God has set before us. We do this by keeping our eyes on Jesus, the champion who initiates and perfects our faith.*

Keep your eyes on Jesus, and take courage from the examples of those who have gone before you.

Promise from God JOB 17:9 | *The righteous keep moving forward, and those with clean hands become stronger and stronger.*

PLEASURE

What gives God pleasure?

JOB 1:8 | *The LORD asked Satan, "Have you noticed my servant Job? He is the finest man in all the earth. He is blameless—a man of complete integrity. He fears God and stays away from evil."*

God is pleased when you are faithful to him because it demonstrates your commitment to him.

JOHN 8:29 | *[Jesus said,] "The one who sent me is with me—he has not deserted me. For I always do what pleases him."*

God is pleased when you obey him because it demonstrates your love for him.

HEBREWS 11:5-6 | *It was by faith that Enoch was taken up to heaven without dying—"he disappeared, because God took him." For before he was taken up, he was known as a person who pleased God. And it is impossible to please God without faith.*

God is pleased when you trust him because it demonstrates your faith in him.

EPHESIANS 1:5 | *God decided in advance to adopt us into his own family by bringing us to himself through Jesus Christ. This is what he wanted to do, and it gave him great pleasure.*

It gives God great pleasure to give eternal life to those who come to him through Jesus Christ.

What kinds of pleasures am I free to enjoy?

ECCLESIASTES 2:24 | *I decided there is nothing better than to enjoy food and drink and to find satisfaction in work. Then I realized that these pleasures are from the hand of God.*

1 TIMOTHY 4:4 | *Since everything God created is good, we should not reject any of it but receive it with thanks.*

God intends for you to enjoy the life he gave you and the good things he created for all people.

NEHEMIAH 8:10 | *Nehemiah continued, "Go and celebrate with a feast of rich foods and sweet drinks, and share gifts of food with people who have nothing prepared. This is a sacred day before our Lord."*

It is good to enjoy occasions of celebrating God's goodness and love.

PSALM 127:4-5 | *Children born to a young man are like arrows in a warrior's hands. How joyful is the man whose quiver is full of them!*

God wants you to enjoy the blessing of your family.

PSALM 16:5, 11 | *LORD, you alone are my inheritance, my cup of blessing. . . . You will show me the way of life, granting me the joy of your presence and the pleasures of living with you forever.*

God wants you to take pleasure in him because he has planned so many blessings for you.

What kinds of pleasures are wrong?

ISAIAH 5:11-12 | *What sorrow for those who get up early in the morning looking for a drink of alcohol and spend long evenings drinking wine to make themselves flaming drunk. They furnish wine and lovely music at their grand parties—lyre and harp, tambourine and flute—but they never think about the LORD or notice what he is doing.*

Pleasures that go against right living or that ignore God and his work in your life and the world around you are wrong.

GALATIANS 5:19, 21 | *When you follow the desires of your sinful nature, the results are very clear: sexual immorality, impurity,* *lustful pleasures. . . . Let me tell you again, as I have before, that anyone living that sort of life will not inherit the Kingdom of God.*

Pleasure that involves sin leads to eternal destruction.

Promise from God PSALM 4:7 | *[God has] given me greater joy than those who have abundant harvests of grain and new wine.*

POVERTY

Does God care that I'm poor? It seems as if other people have everything they need, but I'm struggling to get by.

ISAIAH 25:4 | *You are a tower of refuge to the poor, O LORD, a tower of refuge to the needy in distress. You are a refuge from the storm and a shelter from the heat.*

HEBREWS 13:5 | *Don't love money; be satisfied with what you have. For God has said, "I will never fail you. I will never abandon you."*

If you are poor, your greatest anticipation as a believer is that this condition is temporary. God promises that you will be free from all trouble, including struggling with finances, when you live with him in heaven for eternity. You may not understand why some people seem to get all the breaks here on earth, but God assures you that those who love him will get all the breaks in heaven.

Does God really care about the poor?

PSALM 72:12 | *He will rescue the poor when they cry to him; he will help the oppressed, who have no one to defend them.*

PSALM 102:17 | *He will listen to the prayers of the destitute. He will not reject their pleas.*

PSALM 113:6-8 | *He stoops to look down on heaven and on earth. He lifts the poor from the dust and the needy from the garbage dump. He sets them among princes, even the princes of his own people!*

God cares deeply for the poor.

What is my responsibility to the poor?

PROVERBS 19:17 | *If you help the poor, you are lending to the LORD—and he will repay you!*

ISAIAH 58:10 | *Feed the hungry, and help those in trouble. Then your light will shine out from the darkness, and the darkness around you will be as bright as noon.*

MATTHEW 7:12 | *Do to others whatever you would like them to do to you.*

God has compassion for the poor, so if you want to please God, you also must have compassion for the poor. If your attempts to be caring do not reach as far as your checkbook or your to-do list, your "compassion" is counterfeit. Helping the poor is not merely an obligation but a privilege that brings the joy of helping others as well as reward from God himself.

Promise from God PSALM 41:1 | *Oh, the joys of those who are kind to the poor! The LORD rescues them when they are in trouble.*

POWER

•◀●

How can I have spiritual power?

ACTS 1:8 | *You will receive power when the Holy Spirit comes upon you.*

2 TIMOTHY 1:7 | *God has not given us a spirit of fear and timidity, but of power, love, and self-discipline.*

Spiritual power comes from God alone.

2 CORINTHIANS 12:9 | *Each time [the Lord] said, "My grace is all you need. My power works best in weakness." So now I am glad to boast about my weaknesses, so that the power of Christ can work through me.*

The more you recognize your weaknesses and limitations, the more God's power can work in you. Your weaknesses provide opportunities for God to exercise his power in your work for him.

JOHN 15:5 | *[Jesus said,] "Yes, I am the vine; you are the branches. Those who remain in me, and I in them, will produce much fruit. For apart from me you can do nothing."*

Spiritual power comes from living in fellowship with Jesus Christ. God gives strength to those who are fully committed to him.

How does God exercise his power?

PSALM 65:6 | *You formed the mountains by your power and armed yourself with mighty strength.*

JEREMIAH 10:12 | *God made the earth by his power, and he preserves it by his wisdom. With his own understanding he stretched out the heavens.*

HEBREWS 1:3 | *The Son radiates God's own glory and expresses the very character of God, and he sustains everything by the mighty power of his command.*

God exercised his power in creating the universe and everything in it, and he sustains it by his power.

LUKE 12:5 | *I'll tell you whom to fear. Fear God, who has the power to kill you and then throw you into hell.*

By his power, God will carry out his judgment.

MATTHEW 9:6 | *"I will prove to you that the Son of Man has the authority on earth to forgive sins." Then Jesus turned to the paralyzed man and said, "Stand up, pick up your mat, and go home!"*

God uses his authority to forgive sins and power to heal people.

JOHN 10:28-30 | *[Jesus said,] "I give them eternal life, and they will never perish. No one can snatch them away from me, for my Father has given them to me, and he is more powerful than anyone else. No one can snatch them from the Father's hand. The Father and I are one."*

By his power, Jesus gives eternal life to his followers.

Promise from God **1 PETER 1:5** | *Through your faith, God is protecting you by his power until you receive this salvation, which is ready to be revealed on the last day for all to see.*

PRAYER

What is prayer?

PSALM 145:18 | *The LORD is close to all who call on him, yes, to all who call on him in truth.*

Prayer is conversation with God. It is simply talking with God and listening to him, honestly telling him your thoughts and feelings, praising him, thanking him, confessing your sins, and asking for his help and advice. The essence of prayer is humbly entering into the very presence of almighty God.

PSALM 38:18 | *I confess my sins; I am deeply sorry for what I have done.*

1 JOHN 1:9 | *If we confess our sins to him, he is faithful and just to forgive us our sins and to cleanse us from all wickedness.*

Prayer includes confession of sin, which demonstrates the humility necessary for open lines of communication with the almighty, holy God.

1 SAMUEL 14:36 | *The priest said, "Let's ask God first."*

2 SAMUEL 5:19 | *David asked the LORD, "Should I go out to fight the Philistines?"*

Prayer is asking God for guidance. Then wait for his direction and leading.

PSALM 9:1-2 | *I will praise you, LORD, with all my heart. . . . I will sing praises to your name, O Most High.*

Prayer involves praising your mighty God.

Does the Bible teach a "right way" to pray?

1 SAMUEL 23:2 | *David asked the LORD, "Should I go . . . ?"*

NEHEMIAH 1:4 | *For days I mourned, fasted, and prayed to the God of heaven.*

PSALM 18:1 | *I love you, LORD; you are my strength.*

PSALM 32:5 | *Finally, I confessed all my sins to you and stopped trying to hide my guilt. I said to myself, "I will confess my rebellion to the LORD." And you forgave me! All my guilt is gone.*

EPHESIANS 6:18 | *Pray in the Spirit at all times and on every occasion. Stay alert and be persistent in your prayers for all believers everywhere.*

Throughout the Bible, effective prayer includes elements such as adoration, fasting, confession, making requests, and persistence.

MATTHEW 6:9 | *Pray like this: Our Father, . . .*

In the verses that follow this one, Jesus taught his disciples that prayer is an intimate conversation with the Father that expresses one's dependency on him for daily needs, commitment to obedience, and desire for forgiveness of sins.

LUKE 18:1 | *One day Jesus told his disciples a story to show that they should always pray and never give up.*

We are to be consistent and persistent in prayer.

NEHEMIAH 2:4-5 | *The king asked, "Well, how can I help you?" With a prayer to the God of heaven, I replied . . .*

Prayer can be spontaneous.

Does God always answer prayer?

GENESIS 30:17 | *God answered Leah's prayers. She became pregnant again and gave birth to a fifth son for Jacob.*

PSALM 116:1-2 | *I love the LORD because he hears my voice and my prayer for mercy. Because he bends down to listen, I will pray as long as I have breath!*

God listens carefully to every prayer and answers it. His answer may be yes, no, or wait, just as any loving parent might answer a child. Answering yes to every request would spoil you and endanger your well-being. Answering no to every request would be vindictive and stingy and would dampen your spirit. Answering wait to every prayer would be frustrating. God always answers prayer based on what he knows is best. When you don't get the answer you want, you will grow in spiritual maturity as you accept in faith that God's answer is best.

2 CORINTHIANS 12:8-9 | *Three different times I begged the Lord to take [the thorn in my flesh] away. Each time he said, "My grace is all you need. My power works best in weakness."*

Sometimes, like Paul, you will find that God answers prayer by allowing you to be a shining vessel of God's grace and power.

EXODUS 14:15 | *The LORD said to Moses, "Why are you crying out to me? Tell the people to get moving!"*

Effective prayer is accompanied by a willingness to obey. When God opens a door, walk through it!

Promise from God   2 CHRONICLES 7:14 | *If my people who are called by my name will humble themselves and pray and seek my face and turn from their wicked ways, I will hear from heaven and will forgive their sins and restore their land.*

PREJUDICE

What does the Bible say about ethnic or racial prejudice?

GALATIANS 2:12-14 | *When [Peter] first arrived, he ate with the Gentile Christians, who were not circumcised. But afterward, when some friends of James came, Peter wouldn't eat with the Gentiles anymore. He was afraid of criticism from these people who insisted on the necessity of circumcision. As a result, other Jewish Christians followed Peter's hypocrisy, and even Barnabas was led astray by their hypocrisy. When I saw that they were not following the truth of the gospel message, I said to Peter in front of all the others, "Since you, a Jew by birth, have discarded the Jewish laws and are living like a Gentile, why are you now trying to make these Gentiles follow the Jewish traditions?"*

Any form of prejudice is inconsistent with the Good News we bring about Jesus Christ.

DEUTERONOMY 10:19 | *You, too, must show love to foreigners, for you yourselves were once foreigners in the land of Egypt.*

God wants you to show his love toward those who are different from you, whether it be gender, race, skin color, personality, status, political viewpoint, or some other form of prejudice.

JOHN 1:46 | *"Nazareth!" exclaimed Nathanael. "Can anything good come from Nazareth?" "Come and see for yourself," Philip replied.*

Jesus broke the judgmental stereotypes of his time.

JOHN 4:9 | *The woman was surprised, for Jews refuse to have anything to do with Samaritans. She said to Jesus, "You are a Jew, and I am a Samaritan woman. Why are you asking me for a drink?"*

Jesus reached across the lines of racial and gender prejudice to demonstrate equality and respect for all people.

ACTS 10:28 | *Peter told them, "You know it is against our laws for a Jewish man to enter a Gentile home like this or to associate with you. But God has shown me that I should no longer think of anyone as impure or unclean."*

God wants you to consider whether you have any prejudices. Remember that all the goodness of God is available equally to all people.

Promise from God GALATIANS 3:28 | *There is no longer Jew or Gentile, slave or free, male and female. For you are all one in Christ Jesus.*

PRIDE

Why is pride considered one of the "seven deadly sins," even though other things seem so much worse?

EZEKIEL 28:17 | *Your heart was filled with pride because of all your beauty.*

The Bible indicates that pride was the sin that caused Lucifer (Satan) to be cast from heaven. If selfish pride is strong enough to rip an angel away from the very presence of God, it is certainly strong enough to cause damage in your own life.

PSALM 10:4 | *The wicked are too proud to seek God. They seem to think that God is dead.*

Pride leads to ignoring God and a life of disobedience.

2 TIMOTHY 3:2-4 | *People will love only themselves and their money. They will be boastful and proud. . . . They will be unloving and unforgiving. . . . They will betray their friends, be reckless, be puffed up with pride, and love pleasure rather than God.*

Pride can destroy relationships faster than almost anything else. It can cause you to elevate yourself at the expense of others.

2 CHRONICLES 26:16 | *When [Uzziah] had become powerful, he also became proud, which led to his downfall.*

An inflated estimation of your past successes leads to prideful behavior and, ultimately, judgment.

OBADIAH 1:3 | *You have been deceived by your own pride because you live in a rock fortress and make your home high in the mountains.*

Pride finds comfort in false security.

1 CORINTHIANS 4:6 | *If you pay attention to what I have quoted from the Scriptures, you won't be proud of one of your leaders at the expense of another.*

Pride can infect your spiritual life and divide the church.

ACTS 12:23 | *Instantly, an angel of the Lord struck Herod with a sickness, because he accepted the people's worship instead of giving the glory to God.*

God hates pride and will judge it severely.

Is pride ever healthy and appropriate?

ROMANS 15:17 | *[Paul said,] "I have reason to be enthusiastic about all Christ Jesus has done through me in my service to God."*

It is appropriate to feel satisfaction in what God does through you.

GALATIANS 6:14 | *As for me, may I never boast about anything except the cross of our Lord Jesus Christ.*

Pride is appropriate when it expresses itself in gratefulness to God for his gifts. When you look at your spouse or your children or your talents, and your heart wells up with gratitude to God, he is pleased. Then your focus is on him and not on yourself and your interests.

Promise from God PROVERBS 16:18 | *Pride goes before destruction, and haughtiness before a fall.*

PRIORITIES

What should be my highest priorities?

MARK 12:29-31 | *Jesus replied, "The most important commandment is this: 'Listen, O Israel! The LORD our God is the one and only LORD. And you must love the LORD your God with all your heart, all your soul, all your mind, and all your strength.'*

The second is equally important: 'Love your neighbor as yourself.' No other commandment is greater than these."

Jesus clearly stated the two greatest priorities for every person: to love God and others and to do this with all you've got. When you sincerely love God, you will then love others, too.

How can I tell if God is really my first priority?

EXODUS 20:3 | *You must not have any other god but me.*

DEUTERONOMY 10:12-13 | *What does the LORD your God require of you? He requires only that you fear the LORD your God, and live in a way that pleases him, and love him and serve him with all your heart and soul. And you must always obey the LORD's commands and decrees that I am giving you today for your own good.*

LUKE 12:34 | *Wherever your treasure is, there the desires of your heart will also be.*

If God is the center of your life, you will determine that your relationship with him will be your highest priority. You will long to spend time with him, to talk to him, to listen to him, to think about him often, to please him, and to obey his Word. Your heart will yearn for him, and it's your heart that really matters to God.

Should the pursuit of money or material things be a priority?

PROVERBS 23:4 | *Don't wear yourself out trying to get rich. Be wise enough to know when to quit.*

PROVERBS 27:24 | *Riches don't last forever, and the crown might not be passed to the next generation.*

1 TIMOTHY 6:9 | *People who long to be rich fall into temptation and are trapped by many foolish and harmful desires that plunge them into ruin and destruction.*

You should pursue those things that last the longest and strengthen life the most. The Lord will be around forever, long after material things have disappeared! He will give you greater joy than riches ever could.

Promise from God MATTHEW 6:33 | *Seek the Kingdom of God above all else, and live righteously, and he will give you everything you need.*

PROFANITY

Why is profanity such a big deal?

PHILIPPIANS 4:8 | *Fix your thoughts on what is true, and honorable, and right, and pure, and lovely, and admirable. Think about things that are excellent and worthy of praise.*

What you say shows everyone what is in your heart and mind. When foul language comes out of you, it indicates there is impurity inside you. Your heart and mind should be filled with the good, not the profane.

EXODUS 20:7 | *You must not misuse the name of the LORD your God.*

To use the name of God frivolously is to violate God's standard for holiness. It shows lack of respect and reverence for him. This is important enough that God made it one of the Ten Commandments.

EXODUS 21:15, 17 | *Anyone who strikes father or mother must be put to death. . . . Anyone who dishonors father or mother must be put to death.*

The Bible says that to dishonor your parents is as serious an offense as doing them physical harm.

EPHESIANS 5:4 | *Obscene stories, foolish talk, and coarse jokes— these are not for you. Instead, let there be thankfulness to God.*

Your words show what kind of person you really are. Criticism, gossip, flattery, lying, and profanity are not only "word problems" but are "heart problems" as well. Foul language should not be part of a believer's vocabulary.

TITUS 2:8 | *Teach the truth so that your teaching can't be criticized.*

Your speech should be pure so it cannot be criticized by unbelievers.

Promise from God PSALM 34:12-13 | *Does anyone want to live a life that is long and prosperous? Then keep your tongue from speaking evil and your lips from telling lies!*

PURPOSE

What is my true purpose in life?

JOHN 17:1, 4 | *Jesus looked up to heaven and said, "Father, . . . I brought glory to you here on earth by completing the work you gave me to do."*

ROMANS 11:36 | *Everything comes from him and exists by his power and is intended for his glory.*

Your purpose in life is to honor, obey, and praise God.

MATTHEW 28:18-20 | *Jesus came and told his disciples, "I have been given all authority in heaven and on earth. Therefore, go and make disciples of all the nations, baptizing them in the name of the Father and the Son and the Holy Spirit. Teach these new disciples to obey all the commands I have given you. And be sure of this: I am with you always, even to the end of the age."*

Part of your purpose includes taking part in fulfilling the great commission to tell others about Jesus and in building the Kingdom of God.

ROMANS 8:29 | *God knew his people in advance, and he chose them to become like his Son.*

Part of your purpose is to become as much like Christ as you can, which prepares you for eternal glory.

Does God have a special purpose for me?

PSALM 57:2 | *I cry out to God Most High, to God who will fulfill his purpose for me.*

God has a general purpose and a specific purpose for you. In general, you have been chosen by God to let the love of Jesus shine through you to make an impact on others. More specifically, God has given you spiritual gifts and wants you to use them to make a unique contribution in your sphere of influence. The more you fulfill your general purpose, the clearer your specific purpose will become.

ACTS 20:24 | *My life is worth nothing to me unless I use it for finishing the work assigned me by the Lord Jesus—the work of telling others the Good News about the wonderful grace of God.*

God has given you work to do in a unique role he created just for you. Part of his purpose for you is to bring the Good News of salvation to all people.

2 TIMOTHY 1:9 | *God saved us and called us to live a holy life. He did this, not because we deserved it, but because that was his plan from before the beginning of time—to show us his grace through Christ Jesus.*

You are called by God to live a holy life and to show the love of Jesus to others by the way you live.

Promise from God ROMANS 12:2 | *Don't copy the behavior and customs of this world, but let God transform you into a new person by changing the way you think. Then you will learn to know God's will for you, which is good and pleasing and perfect.*

RECONCILIATION

What does the Bible say about reconciliation between people?

MATTHEW 5:23-24 | *If you are presenting a sacrifice at the altar in the Temple and you suddenly remember that someone has something against you, leave your sacrifice there at the altar. Go and be reconciled to that person. Then come and offer your sacrifice to God.*

Being reconciled with other people is important to God because it demonstrates a humble spirit, which is essential to healthy relationships.

MATTHEW 5:25-26 | *When you are on the way to court with your adversary, settle your differences quickly. Otherwise, your accuser may hand you over to the judge, who will hand you over to an officer, and you will be thrown into prison. And if that happens, you surely won't be free again until you have paid the last penny.*

Working toward reconciliation with others is important to your own health and peace of mind.

EPHESIANS 2:14 | *Christ himself has brought peace to us. He united Jews and Gentiles into one people when, in his own body on the cross, he broke down the wall of hostility that separated us.*

God, through Christ, has made a way for groups of people in conflict with one another to make peace and be fully reconciled.

How can I be reconciled to God?

COLOSSIANS 1:20-21 | *Through [Christ] God reconciled everything to himself. He made peace with everything in heaven and on earth by means of Christ's blood on the cross. This includes you who were once far away from God.*

COLOSSIANS 2:14 | *He canceled the record of the charges against us and took it away by nailing it to the cross.*

Through the death of Jesus Christ, God has made it possible for you to be reconciled to him.

ROMANS 5:1 | *Since we have been made right in God's sight by faith, we have peace with God because of what Jesus Christ our Lord has done for us.*

You must have faith in what Jesus Christ has done for you in order to be reconciled with God.

Promise from God COLOSSIANS 1:22 | *[God] has reconciled you to himself through the death of Christ in his physical body. As a result, he has brought you into his own presence, and you are holy and blameless as you stand before him without a single fault.*

REGRETS

How can I deal with the regrets of my life?

2 CORINTHIANS 5:17 | *Anyone who belongs to Christ has become a new person. The old life is gone; a new life has begun!*

When you come to faith in Jesus, he forgives your sins— all of them. He forgets your past and gives you a fresh start. You may still have to live with the consequences of your sins, but because God has forgiven you, you can move forward without the feelings of guilt that often accompany regret. Because God no longer holds your sins against you, you no longer have to hold them against yourself. Now you can be free from self-condemnation.

PHILIPPIANS 3:13-14 | *I focus on this one thing: Forgetting the past and looking forward to what lies ahead, I press on.*

Focus on God, who controls the future, not on regrets of the past. The past is over, so don't live a life of what-ifs, feeling angry at yourself for what you did and bitter toward God for allowing you to do it. God doesn't cause regrets; he washes them away when you ask him to walk with you into the future.

Promise from God   2 CORINTHIANS 7:10 | *The kind of sorrow God wants us to experience leads us away from sin and results in salvation. There's no regret for that kind of sorrow.*

REPENTANCE

Is repentance necessary? Why does God want me to repent?

2 CHRONICLES 30:9 | *The L*ORD *your God is gracious and merciful. If you return to him, he will not continue to turn his face from you.*

Repentance is necessary for an ongoing relationship with God. You must turn away from anything that prevents you from worshiping and obeying God wholeheartedly.

JEREMIAH 3:12 | *The L*ORD *says: ". . . Come home to me again, for I am merciful. I will not be angry with you forever."*

Repentance is your only hope of receiving God's mercy. Those who refuse to see and admit their own sins can't be forgiven for them; they have placed themselves outside God's mercy and blessing.

EZEKIEL 18:30-32 | *I will judge each of you, O people of Israel, according to your actions, says the Sovereign L*ORD*. Repent, and turn from your sins. Don't let them destroy you! Put all your rebellion behind you, and find yourselves a new heart* *and a new spirit. For why should you die . . . ? I don't want you to die, says the Sovereign LORD. Turn back and live!*

Repentance literally allows you to receive a new life from God, a life where the very Spirit of God lives within you.

LUKE 24:47 | *There is forgiveness of sins for all who repent.*

Repentance allows you to receive forgiveness for your sins. If you are sincere and humble when you come to God, he will forgive you, no matter how many times you need to ask.

MATTHEW 11:20, 23 | *Jesus began to denounce the towns where he had done so many of his miracles, because they hadn't repented of their sins and turned to God. . . . "And you people of Capernaum, will you be honored in heaven? No, you will go down to the place of the dead. For if the miracles I did for you had been done in wicked Sodom, it would still be here today."*

Refusal to turn away from your sins will bring God's judgment.

LUKE 15:10 | *There is joy in the presence of God's angels when even one sinner repents.*

All heaven rejoices when you repent.

Promise from God 2 CHRONICLES 7:14 | *If my people who are called by my name will humble themselves and pray and seek my face and turn from their wicked ways, I will hear from heaven and will forgive their sins and restore their land.*

REPUTATION

Why should I care about my reputation?

2 CORINTHIANS 8:20 | *We are traveling together to guard against any criticism for the way we are handling this generous gift.*

You should care about having a reputation of integrity so that the credibility of your witness for Christ cannot be questioned by anyone. It is sad when the message of Christ is hindered by a damaged reputation.

MATTHEW 6:1 | *Don't do your good deeds publicly, to be admired.*

Jesus warns against pursuing a good reputation just to impress others.

What are some elements of a good reputation?

2 PETER 1:5-7 | *Make every effort to respond to God's promises. Supplement your faith with a generous provision of moral excellence, and moral excellence with knowledge, and knowledge with self-control, and self-control with patient endurance, and patient endurance with godliness, and godliness with brotherly affection, and brotherly affection with love for everyone.*

Any reputation you achieve should result from being fully committed to building spiritual character in your life.

How can I develop a good reputation?

1 PETER 2:12 | *Be careful to live properly among your unbelieving neighbors. Then even if they accuse you of doing wrong,*

they will see your honorable behavior, and they will give honor to God when he judges the world.

The surest way to influence the way others think of you is through consistent godly behavior.

DEUTERONOMY 4:6 | *Obey [the commands of the Lord] completely, and you will display your wisdom and intelligence among the surrounding nations. When they hear all these decrees, they will exclaim, "How wise and prudent are the people of this great nation!"*

Obedience to God results in a reputation for wisdom and intelligence.

MARK 2:16 | *When the teachers of religious law who were Pharisees saw [Jesus] eating with tax collectors and other sinners, they asked his disciples, "Why does he eat with such scum?"*

Jesus doesn't look at your past reputation. His love can transform you, no matter what you've done.

3 JOHN 1:3 | *Some of the traveling teachers recently returned and made me very happy by telling me about your faithfulness and that you are living according to the truth.*

You can earn a good reputation by living according to God's standards of purity and truth.

Promise from God 1 PETER 5:6 | *Humble yourselves under the mighty power of God, and at the right time he will lift you up in honor.*

RESPECT

—————————————————————————— •◄•

To whom should I show respect?

EXODUS 3:5 | *"Do not come any closer,"* the LORD warned. *"Take off your sandals, for you are standing on holy ground."*

1 SAMUEL 12:24 | *Be sure to fear the LORD and faithfully serve him.*

Respect God above everyone else.

EXODUS 20:12 | *Honor your father and mother. Then you will live a long, full life in the land the LORD your God is giving you.*

Your parents deserve deep respect, for they were chosen by God to be the ones to raise and teach you.

ROMANS 13:1-2 | *Everyone must submit to governing authorities. For all authority comes from God, and those in positions of authority have been placed there by God. So anyone who rebels against authority is rebelling against what God has instituted.*

Those in authority over you deserve your respect. Even if they are evil or oppressive, you must respect their position of authority. Someday you may be in their position and will want the respect of those under you.

1 THESSALONIANS 5:12-13 | *Honor those who are your leaders in the Lord's work. . . . Show them great respect and wholehearted love because of their work.*

Spiritual leaders should be treated with respect.

LEVITICUS 19:32 | *Stand up in the presence of the elderly, and show respect for the aged.*

Show respect for the elderly.

EPHESIANS 6:5, 9 | *Slaves, obey your earthly masters with deep respect and fear. Serve them sincerely as you would serve Christ. . . . Masters, treat your slaves in the same way. Don't threaten them; remember, you both have the same Master in heaven, and he has no favorites.*

Employers and employees should treat each other with respect.

ROMANS 12:10 | *Love each other with genuine affection, and take delight in honoring each other.*

1 PETER 2:17 | *Respect everyone, and love your Christian brothers and sisters. Fear God, and respect the king.*

Treat all people with respect.

How can I show respect to God?

DEUTERONOMY 10:12 | *What does the LORD your God require of you? He requires only that you fear the LORD your God, and live in a way that pleases him, and love him and serve him with all your heart and soul.*

HEBREWS 12:28-29 | *Since we are receiving a Kingdom that is unshakable, let us be thankful and please God by worshiping him with holy fear and awe. For our God is a devouring fire.*

Show your respect and awe for God by serving and worshiping him with reverence.

ECCLESIASTES 5:1 | *As you enter the house of God, keep your ears open and your mouth shut.*

HABAKKUK 2:20 | *The LORD is in his holy Temple. Let all the earth be silent before him.*

Keeping silent in God's presence shows respect for him.

LEVITICUS 22:32 | *Do not bring shame on my holy name, for I will display my holiness among the people. . . . I am the LORD who makes you holy.*

Respect for God means you show reverence for his name.

ACTS 10:2 | *[Cornelius] was a devout, God-fearing man, as was everyone in his household. He gave generously to the poor and prayed regularly to God.*

Generous giving is a way to show your reverence for God.

Promise from God PSALM 25:12, 14 | *Who are those who fear the LORD? He will show them the path they should choose. . . . The LORD is a friend to those who fear him. He teaches them his covenant.*

RESPONSIBILITY

Why is responsibility an important character trait?

GENESIS 39:2-3 | *The LORD was with Joseph, so he succeeded in everything he did as he served in the home of his Egyptian master. Potiphar noticed this and realized that the LORD was with Joseph, giving him success in everything he did.*

GENESIS 41:41 | *Pharaoh said to Joseph, "I hereby put you in charge of the entire land of Egypt."*

Responsibility can open doors of opportunity. If you are responsible with what you are given, greater opportunities and more responsibility will come your way.

JEREMIAH 31:30 | *All people will die for their own sins.*

EZEKIEL 18:20 | *The person who sins is the one who will die.*

GALATIANS 6:5 | *We are each responsible for our own conduct.*

Responsibility is important because you will be held accountable for your own actions. You cannot blame others for what you choose to do.

What are some things for which I am responsible?

GENESIS 2:15 | *The LORD God placed the man in the Garden of Eden to tend and watch over it.*

PSALM 8:4-6 | *What are mere mortals that you should think about them . . . ? Yet you made them only a little lower than God. . . . You gave them charge of everything you made, putting all things under their authority.*

You are responsible for the care of God's creation.

GENESIS 43:8-9 | *Judah said to his father, "Send the boy with me, and we will be on our way. . . . I personally guarantee his safety. You may hold me responsible if I don't bring him back to you."*

You are responsible for keeping your promises.

EXODUS 21:19 | *If he is later able to walk outside again, even with a crutch, the assailant will not be punished but must compensate his victim for lost wages and provide for his full recovery.*

You are responsible to compensate others for any injury or harm you caused them.

MATTHEW 12:37 | *The words you say will either acquit you or condemn you.*

You are responsible for the words you speak.

1 KINGS 1:6 | *His father, King David, had never disciplined him at any time, even by asking, "Why are you doing that?"*

You are responsible for disciplining your children.

JOHN 12:48 | *All who reject me and my message will be judged on the day of judgment by the truth I have spoken.*

You are responsible for how you respond to Jesus and his message of salvation.

Promise from God MATTHEW 25:29 | *To those who use well what they are given, even more will be given, and they will have an abundance. But from those who do nothing, even what little they have will be taken away.*

RESTLESSNESS

Is it wrong to feel restless?

NUMBERS 20:7-8, 11 | *The LORD said to Moses, ". . . As the people watch, speak to the rock over there, and it will pour out its water." . . . Then Moses raised his hand and struck the rock twice with the staff.*

Restlessness rooted in impatience can lead to sin.

1 SAMUEL 13:12 | *I felt compelled to offer the burnt offering myself before you came.*

When you are so restless that you disregard God's way in favor of your own, you are more likely to cut corners and displease God.

ECCLESIASTES 1:13; 12:13 | *I devoted myself to search for understanding and to explore by wisdom everything being done under heaven. . . . Here now is my final conclusion: Fear God and obey his commands, for this is everyone's duty.*

A restlessness that searches for truth can lead to a deeper understanding of God and his purposes.

How do I find peace?

MATTHEW 11:28 | *Jesus said, "Come to me, all of you who are weary and carry heavy burdens, and I will give you rest."*

Jesus promises his peace to all who come to him in faith.

ROMANS 5:1 | *Since we have been made right in God's sight by faith, we have peace with God because of what Jesus Christ our Lord has done for us.*

Knowing your eternal destiny gives you deep peace and security.

PHILIPPIANS 4:6-7 | *Don't worry about anything; instead, pray about everything. . . . Then you will experience God's peace, which exceeds anything we can understand. His peace will guard your hearts and minds as you live in Christ Jesus.*

Being in constant communication with the God of peace gives you peace.

Promise from God ISAIAH 43:2 | *When you go through deep waters, I will be with you. When you go through rivers of difficulty, you will not drown.*

SACRIFICE

Why did people sacrifice animals in the Old Testament?

LEVITICUS 10:17 | *The LORD has given [the sin offering] to you to remove the guilt of the community and to purify the people, making them right with the LORD.*

HEBREWS 9:22 | *Without the shedding of blood, there is no forgiveness.*

In order for sins to be atoned for and forgiven, death— the shedding of blood—is required. Before Jesus came to earth and shed his blood, animal sacrifice fulfilled this function.

EXODUS 12:3, 23 | *Announce to the whole community of Israel that on the tenth day of this month each family must choose a lamb or a young goat for a sacrifice. . . . For the LORD will pass through the land to strike down the Egyptians. But when he sees the blood on the top and sides of the doorframe, the LORD will pass over your home. He will not permit his death angel to enter your house and strike you down.*

Animals were used as substitutes so that human blood would not be shed.

PSALM 50:5 | *Bring my faithful people to me—those who made a covenant with me by giving sacrifices.*

Sacrifice was the way people showed their covenant relationship with God.

What is the significance of Christ's sacrifice?

JOHN 1:29 | *John saw Jesus coming toward him and said, "Look! The Lamb of God who takes away the sin of the world!"*

ROMANS 3:25 | *God presented Jesus as the sacrifice for sin. People are made right with God when they believe that Jesus sacrificed his life, shedding his blood.*

God sent Jesus to take the punishment for your sins and to satisfy God's anger against you. You are made right with God when you believe that Jesus shed his blood and sacrificed his life for you.

1 PETER 2:24 | *He personally carried our sins in his body on the cross so that we can be dead to sin and live for what is right. By his wounds you are healed.*

Jesus Christ took the punishment you deserve for your sins and made atonement for you—that is, made you "at one" with God—not by covering up your sins but by taking them away.

MATTHEW 26:26-28 | *As they were eating, Jesus took some bread and blessed it. Then he broke it in pieces and gave it to the disciples, saying, "Take this and eat it, for this is my body." And he took a cup of wine and gave thanks to God for it. He gave it to them and said, "Each of you drink from it, for this is my blood, which confirms the covenant between God and his people. It is poured out as a sacrifice to forgive the sins of many."*

Jesus' death began a new covenant between God and those who come to him by faith. Now you can have an intimate relationship with God because Jesus removed your sin by his sacrificial death.

ROMANS 8:3 | *The law of Moses was unable to save us because of the weakness of our sinful nature. So God did what the law could not do. He sent his own Son in a body like the bodies we sinners have. And in that body God declared an end to sin's control over us by giving his Son as a sacrifice for our sins.*

Animal sacrifices could not take away your sin; only Jesus' sacrifice for you could take away your sin and make it possible for you to have eternal life.

JOHN 3:16 | *God loved the world so much that he gave his one and only Son, so that everyone who believes in him will not perish but have eternal life.*

JOHN 14:6 | *Jesus told him, "I am the way, the truth, and the life. No one can come to the Father except through me."*

ACTS 4:12 | *There is salvation in no one else! God has given no other name under heaven by which we must be saved.*

1 TIMOTHY 2:5 | *There is only one God and one Mediator who can reconcile God and humanity—the man Christ Jesus.*

Because Jesus is the only means by which forgiveness can be obtained, faith in him is the only means of salvation.

What kinds of sacrifices am I called on to make?

ROMANS 12:1 | *I plead with you to give your bodies to God because of all he has done for you. Let them be a living and holy sacrifice—the kind he will find acceptable. This is truly the way to worship him.*

God wants you to give him your whole life, even if it means sacrificing comfort or pleasure.

HEBREWS 13:15 | *Let us offer through Jesus a continual sacrifice of praise to God, proclaiming our allegiance to his name.*

When you praise God, you are offering him a pleasing sacrifice.

EPHESIANS 5:2 | *Live a life filled with love, following the example of Christ. He loved us and offered himself as a sacrifice for us, a pleasing aroma to God.*

HEBREWS 13:16 | *Don't forget to do good and to share with those in need. These are the sacrifices that please God.*

Just as Jesus gave himself for you, he wants you to give yourself in service to other people—even to the point of giving your life for them if necessary.

Promise from God HEBREWS 9:27-28 | *Just as each person is destined to die once and after that comes judgment, so also Christ died once for all time as a sacrifice to take away the sins of many people. He will come again, not to deal with our sins, but to bring salvation to all who are eagerly waiting for him.*

SALVATION

What does it mean to be saved?

ROMANS 3:24 | *God, with undeserved kindness, declares that we are righteous. He did this through Christ Jesus when he freed us from the penalty for our sins.*

ROMANS 4:7-8 | *Oh, what joy for those whose disobedience is forgiven, whose sins are put out of sight. Yes, what joy for those whose record the Lord has cleared of sin.*

Being saved means your sins, which meant an eternal death sentence, no longer count against you. Instead, they are forgiven by the grace of God, and you are given the free gift of eternal life. Being saved does not spare you from earthly troubles, but it does spare you from eternal judgment.

PSALM 103:12 | *He has removed our sins as far from us as the east is from the west.*

Being saved means your sins have been completely forgiven by God.

PSALM 51:9-10 | *Remove the stain of my guilt. Create in me a clean heart, O God.*

Being saved means the stain of guilt has been washed away. Your guilt is gone—you are given a clean slate!

1 PETER 2:10 | *Once you had no identity as a people; now you are God's people. Once you received no mercy; now you have received God's mercy.*

Being saved means you have received mercy from God.

JOHN 10:28-29 | *[Jesus said,] "I give them eternal life, and they will never perish. No one can snatch them away from me, for my Father has given them to me, and he is more powerful than anyone else. No one can snatch them from the Father's hand."*

Being saved means you are assured of living forever in heaven. You will live on the new earth, where there will no longer be sin, pain, or suffering.

How can I be saved?

ROMANS 10:13 | *Everyone who calls on the name of the LORD will be saved.*

God's Word promises salvation to anyone who comes to God and repents. Call out to him and tell him you need him to save you. He promises he will.

JOHN 3:16 | *God loved the world so much that he gave his one and only Son, so that everyone who believes in him will not perish but have eternal life.*

JOHN 5:24 | *[Jesus said,] "I tell you the truth, those who listen to my message and believe in God who sent me have eternal life. They will never be condemned for their sins, but they have already passed from death into life."*

Jesus himself promised that if you believe in him, you will be saved.

ROMANS 10:9-10 | *If you confess with your mouth that Jesus is Lord and believe in your heart that God raised him from the dead, you will be saved. For it is by believing in your heart that you are made right with God, and it is by confessing with your mouth that you are saved.*

EPHESIANS 2:8 | *God saved you by his grace when you believed. And you can't take credit for this; it is a gift from God.*

It seems too easy. The greatest gift God could ever offer—life in a perfect world forever—is absolutely free. You just have to accept the gift by agreeing with God that you are a sinner, acknowledging that your sin has cut you off from God; accepting Jesus' death on the cross as a sacrifice to pay the penalty for your sin; and believing that Jesus is Lord over everything because he is the Son of God. Then the gift is yours.

Is salvation available to anyone?

LUKE 2:11 | *The Savior—yes, the Messiah, the Lord—has been born today in Bethlehem, the city of David!*

Jesus was born in a humble stable among very ordinary people to powerfully demonstrate that salvation is available to anyone who sincerely seeks him.

JOHN 3:16 | *God loved the world so much that he gave his one and only Son, so that everyone who believes in him will not perish but have eternal life.*

Jesus promised that those who believe in him will be saved. The only thing people have to do is accept what Jesus did for them.

HEBREWS 9:27 | *Each person is destined to die once and after that comes judgment.*

REVELATION 20:12 | *I saw the dead, both great and small, standing before God's throne. And the books were opened, including the Book of Life. And the dead were judged according to what they had done, as recorded in the books.*

Salvation is available to all, but a time will come when it will be too late to receive it.

How can I be sure of my salvation?

JOHN 1:12 | *To all who believed him and accepted him, he gave the right to become children of God.*

Just as a child cannot be "unborn," God's children—those who believe in Jesus Christ—cannot lose their salvation."

ROMANS 8:14 | *All who are led by the Spirit of God are children of God.*

The Holy Spirit takes up residence in your heart when you become God's child.

How does salvation affect my daily life?

2 CORINTHIANS 5:17 | *Anyone who belongs to Christ has become a new person. The old life is gone; a new life has begun!*

Salvation gives you hope not only for eternity but also for today. You have been given a new life and new power for living.

ROMANS 6:6-9 | *We know that our old sinful selves were crucified with Christ so that sin might lose its power in our lives. We are no longer slaves to sin. For when we died with Christ we were set free from the power of sin. And since we died with Christ, we know we will also live with him. We are sure of this because Christ was raised from the dead, and he will never die again. Death no longer has any power over him.*

Salvation brings you freedom from the power of sin and freedom to live a new life.

ROMANS 5:1 | *Since we have been made right in God's sight by faith, we have peace with God because of what Jesus Christ our Lord has done for us.*

Salvation brings peace with God.

EPHESIANS 2:10 | *He has created us anew in Christ Jesus, so we can do the good things he planned for us long ago.*

God created you for a purpose. Salvation enables you to fulfill that purpose by the power of God at work within you.

Promise from God ROMANS 10:9 | *If you confess with your mouth that Jesus is Lord and believe in your heart that God raised him from the dead, you will be saved.*

SEDUCTION

How can I avoid being seduced into doing wrong?

GENESIS 39:10 | *[Potiphar's wife] kept putting pressure on Joseph day after day, but he refused to sleep with her, and he kept out of her way as much as possible.*

Determine in your heart that you will not do evil. If someone is trying to seduce you, stay away from that person as much as possible!

GENESIS 39:11-12 | *One day, however, no one else was around when he went in to do his work. She came and grabbed him by his cloak, demanding, "Come on, sleep with me!" Joseph tore himself away, but he left his cloak in her hand as he ran from the house.*

PROVERBS 5:7-8 | *My sons, listen to me. Never stray from what I am about to say: Stay away from her! Don't go near the door of her house!*

Run away from temptation as fast as you can! Sometimes it's not enough to simply ignore a situation; you must remove yourself from it.

PROVERBS 4:23 | *Guard your heart above all else, for it determines the course of your life.*

Don't let yourself become emotionally intimate with a woman who is not your wife.

1 JOHN 2:26 | *I am writing these things to warn you about those who want to lead you astray.*

Study God's Word in order to keep from being seduced by those who teach falsehood.

Promise from God ECCLESIASTES 7:26 | *I discovered that a seductive woman is a trap more bitter than death. Her passion is a snare, and her soft hands are chains. Those who are pleasing to God will escape her, but sinners will be caught in her snare.*

SELF-CONTROL

What are some ways to develop self-control?

PSALM 119:9 | *How can a young person stay pure? By obeying your word.*

2 TIMOTHY 2:5 | *Athletes cannot win the prize unless they follow the rules.*

To develop self-control, you first need to know God's guidelines for right living as found in the Bible. Reading God's

Word consistently—preferably every day—keeps his guidelines for right living fresh in your mind.

PSALM 141:3 | *Take control of what I say, O LORD, and guard my lips.*

MATTHEW 12:36 | *You must give an account on judgment day for every idle word you speak.*

JAMES 1:26 | *If you claim to be religious but don't control your tongue, you are fooling yourself, and your religion is worthless.*

You exercise self-control by watching what you say. How often do you wish you could take back your words as soon as they have left your mouth?

ROMANS 13:14 | *Clothe yourself with the presence of the Lord Jesus Christ. And don't let yourself think about ways to indulge your evil desires.*

1 TIMOTHY 4:8 | *Physical training is good, but training for godliness is much better, promising benefits in this life and in the life to come.*

2 PETER 1:5-6 | *Supplement your faith with a generous provision of moral excellence, and moral excellence with knowledge, and knowledge with self-control, and self-control with patient endurance, and patient endurance with godliness.*

Just as a musician or an athlete must develop talent, strength, and coordination through intentional effort, spiritual fitness must be intentional as well. God promises to reward such effort. God wants his people to be disciplined in their habits.

What should I do when I need help beyond my own self-control?

PSALM 60:12 | *With God's help we will do mighty things, for he will trample down our foes.*

PSALM 61:2 | *From the ends of the earth, I cry to you for help when my heart is overwhelmed. Lead me to the towering rock of safety.*

2 CORINTHIANS 12:9 | *[The Lord said,] "My grace is all you need. My power works best in weakness."*

The Bible says that God's power is greatest in your times of weakness. When you face a problem or temptation too big for you to handle, run to God for help and watch his power accomplish more than you could ever do on your own.

1 CORINTHIANS 10:13 | *The temptations in your life are no different from what others experience. And God is faithful. He will not allow the temptation to be more than you can stand. When you are tempted, he will show you a way out so that you can endure.*

Sometimes it is necessary to confess your struggles to a godly friend or counselor so he or she can partner with you in your specific struggle and provide accountability.

Promise from God 2 TIMOTHY 1:7 | *God has . . . given us a spirit of . . . power, love, and self-discipline.*

SENSITIVITY

In what areas might I need to develop more sensitivity?

DEUTERONOMY 15:7 | *If there are any poor . . . in your towns when you arrive in the land the LORD your God is giving you, do not be hard-hearted or tightfisted toward them.*

Try to be sensitive and openhearted to the needs of the poor and oppressed.

PROVERBS 27:14 | *A loud and cheerful greeting early in the morning will be taken as a curse!*

Take special care to be sensitive toward those who are around you every day. They are the ones you are most likely to annoy.

PROVERBS 28:14 | *Blessed are those who fear to do wrong, but the stubborn are headed for serious trouble.*

Be sensitive to sin in your life so that you can keep your conscience clear.

ACTS 13:2-3 | *One day as these men were worshiping the Lord and fasting, the Holy Spirit said, "Dedicate Barnabas and Saul for the special work to which I have called them." So after more fasting and prayer, the men laid their hands on them and sent them on their way.*

ACTS 16:6-7, 9-10 | *Paul and Silas traveled through the area of Phrygia and Galatia, because the Holy Spirit had prevented them from preaching the word in the province of Asia at that time. Then . . . they headed north for the province of Bithynia, but again the Spirit of Jesus did not allow them to go there.*

. . . That night Paul had a vision: A man from Macedonia in northern Greece was standing there, pleading with him, "Come over to Macedonia and help us!" So we decided to leave for Macedonia at once, having concluded that God was calling us to preach the Good News there.

Be sensitive to the leading of the Holy Spirit.

How can I be more sensitive toward my family?

EPHESIANS 5:33 | *Each man must love his wife as he loves himself, and the wife must respect her husband.*

EPHESIANS 6:1-2 | *Children, obey your parents because you belong to the Lord, for this is the right thing to do. "Honor your father and mother." This is the first commandment with a promise.*

COLOSSIANS 3:21 | *Fathers, do not aggravate your children, or they will become discouraged.*

You can be more thoughtful by obeying God's basic guidelines for family roles and responsibilities—love, respect, and honor.

1 THESSALONIANS 2:7 | *As apostles of Christ we certainly had a right to make some demands of you, but instead we were like children among you. Or we were like a mother feeding and caring for her own children.*

You can be more willing to lay aside your own rights and treat your family with gentleness and care.

PROVERBS 12:25 | *Worry weighs a person down; an encouraging word cheers a person up.*

PROVERBS 15:28 | *The heart of the godly thinks carefully before speaking; the mouth of the wicked overflows with evil words.*

EPHESIANS 4:29 | *Don't use foul or abusive language. Let everything you say be good and helpful, so that your words will be an encouragement to those who hear them.*

JAMES 1:19 | *You must all be quick to listen, slow to speak, and slow to get angry.*

You can be thoughtful and encouraging with your words by listening well and thinking before speaking.

Promise from God   EZEKIEL 11:19 | *I will give them singleness of heart and put a new spirit within them. I will take away their stony, stubborn heart and give them a tender, responsive heart.*

SEX/SEXUALITY

What does God think about sex?

GENESIS 1:27-28 | *God created human beings in his own image. In the image of God he created them; male and female he created them. Then God blessed them and said, "Be fruitful and multiply. Fill the earth and govern it."*

GENESIS 2:24 | *A man leaves his father and mother and is joined to his wife, and the two are united into one.*

God created sex. He made men and women sexual beings to reproduce and replenish the next generation and to express love and delight in their spouses. The sexual relationship is a key part of the biblical principle that a husband and wife become one. God intended sex to be a good thing within the context of a marriage relationship.

Is sex in marriage only for reproduction, or did God plan for husbands and wives to enjoy it, to delight in each other through sex?

PROVERBS 5:18-19 | *Rejoice in the wife of your youth. . . . Let her breasts satisfy you always. May you always be captivated by her love.*

EPHESIANS 5:28, 33 | *Husbands ought to love their wives as they love their own bodies. For a man who loves his wife actually shows love for himself. . . . So again I say, each man must love his wife as he loves himself.*

God clearly intends for you to love your wife and delight in having sex with your wife. Sex is not only for reproduction but also for creating a bond of love and enjoyment between husbands and wives.

What rights do a husband and wife have to each other's bodies?

1 CORINTHIANS 7:3 | *The husband should fulfill his wife's sexual needs, and the wife should fulfill her husband's needs.*

Husbands and wives do not completely own their own bodies. When they marry, each mate has a loving claim to the other's body.

Is it really so bad if I think about having sex with someone other than my wife, as long as I don't act on it?

EXODUS 20:17 | *You must not covet your neighbor's house. You must not covet your neighbor's wife.*

MATTHEW 5:27-28 | *[Jesus said,] "You have heard the commandment that says, 'You must not commit adultery.' But I say, anyone who even looks at a woman with lust has already committed adultery with her in his heart."*

Lust is adultery in the heart. When you imagine having sex with someone, you have consummated it in your heart.

Will God forgive my sexual sins?

ACTS 13:38-39 | *Through this man Jesus there is forgiveness for your sins. Everyone who believes in him is declared right with God.*

God will forgive any sin if there is sincere repentance and a desire to stop that sin.

ROMANS 1:24 | *God abandoned them to do whatever shameful things their hearts desired. As a result, they did vile and degrading things with each other's bodies.*

God will not forgive a sin if you persist in it or are not sorry about it. Engaging in persistent, willful sin shows that your repentance is not genuine; you care more about pleasing yourself than pleasing God.

Promise from God   1 CORINTHIANS 6:13 | *You can't say that our bodies were made for sexual immorality. They were made for the Lord, and the Lord cares about our bodies.*

SIN

What is sin?

ROMANS 3:23 | *Everyone has sinned; we all fall short of God's glorious standard.*

Sin is falling short of the standard of purity set forth by God, who is holy.

ROMANS 2:15 | *They demonstrate that God's law is written in their hearts, for their own conscience and thoughts either accuse them or tell them they are doing right.*

Sin is violating God's moral law.

ROMANS 6:12 | *Do not let sin control the way you live; do not give in to sinful desires.*

Sin is a power that seeks to influence, enslave, and destroy you.

ROMANS 7:21-23 | *I have discovered this principle of life—that when I want to do what is right, I inevitably do what is wrong. I love God's law with all my heart. But there is another power within me that is at war with my mind. This power makes me a slave to the sin that is still within me.*

Sin is warfare of the soul, a constant battle that goes on inside you.

JAMES 4:17 | *Remember, it is sin to know what you ought to do and then not do it.*

Sin is not only doing the wrong things but failing to do the right things.

What are the consequences of sin?

ISAIAH 59:2 | *It's your sins that have cut you off from God. Because of your sins, he has turned away and will not listen anymore.*

Sin alienates and separates you from God, preventing you from enjoying a relationship with him.

ROMANS 6:23 | *The wages of sin is death.*

2 THESSALONIANS 1:9 | *They will be punished with eternal destruction, forever separated from the Lord and from his glorious power.*

Sin brings God's punishment because sin is a violation of his laws and holiness. Death is the penalty for sin—eternal judgment by God.

Is everyone sinful?

ECCLESIASTES 7:20 | *Not a single person on earth is always good and never sins.*

ISAIAH 53:6 | *All of us, like sheep, have strayed away. We have left God's paths to follow our own.*

All people have sinned against God. Everyone is born with a sinful nature. It is a condition present at birth, not something that can be avoided with the right training.

JEREMIAH 17:9 | *The human heart is the most deceitful of all things, and desperately wicked. Who really knows how bad it is?*

The human heart is far more sinful than anyone wants to believe.

Is there a way to be free from sin?

ISAIAH 1:18 | *"Come now, let's settle this," says the LORD. "Though your sins are like scarlet, I will make them as white as snow. Though they are red like crimson, I will make them as white as wool."*

MATTHEW 26:28 | *[Jesus said,] "This is my blood, which confirms the covenant between God and his people. It is poured out as a sacrifice to forgive the sins of many."*

2 CORINTHIANS 5:21 | *God made Christ, who never sinned, to be the offering for our sin, so that we could be made right with God through Christ.*

God has made it possible for the stain of your sins to be removed because of the death and resurrection of Jesus Christ. He took the punishment you deserve for your sins so that you can have a relationship with him. When you believe and accept what he did for you, God then looks at you as though you had never sinned.

1 JOHN 1:9 | *If we confess our sins to him, he is faithful and just to forgive us our sins and to cleanse us from all wickedness.*

Confessing your sins to God, turning away from them to obey him, is the only way to be free from sin's power and guilt. When you confess your sins to God, he forgives you and forgets them.

ROMANS 6:6, 18 | *Our old sinful selves were crucified with Christ so that sin might lose its power in our lives. We are no longer slaves to sin. . . . Now you are free from your slavery to sin, and you have become slaves to righteous living.*

Because of Jesus' death and resurrection, those who have faith in him are free from the power of sin. Because sin's power to enslave you has been defeated, you can enlist the Spirit's power to help you fight against temptation.

Am I really a Christian if I still sin?

ROMANS 7:18-20 | *I know that nothing good lives in me, that is, in my sinful nature. I want to do what is right, but I can't. I want to do what is good, but I don't. I don't want to do what is wrong, but I do it anyway. But if I do what I don't want to do, I am not really the one doing wrong; it is sin living in me that does it.*

Though you will always struggle with sin, even after you become a Christian, God has provided a way to gain victory over it.

ROMANS 8:5 | *Those who are dominated by the sinful nature think about sinful things, but those who are controlled by the Holy Spirit think about things that please the Spirit.*

Sin loses its influence over you as you increasingly yield your life to the control of the Holy Spirit. The Spirit of God living in you reduces your appetite for sin and increases your hunger for God.

PSALM 119:11 | *I have hidden your word in my heart, that I might not sin against you.*

God's Word leads you away from sin because it communicates the ways of a holy God to guide you and protect you in life.

Promise from God 1 PETER 2:24 | *[Christ] personally carried our sins in his body on the cross so that we can be dead to sin and live for what is right. By his wounds you are healed.*

SPIRITUAL WARFARE

Is spiritual warfare a reality?

GENESIS 3:1 | *The serpent was the shrewdest of all the wild animals the LORD God had made. One day he asked the woman, "Did God really say you must not eat the fruit from any of the trees in the garden?"*

MATTHEW 4:1 | *Jesus was led by the Spirit into the wilderness to be tempted there by the devil.*

The Bible clearly teaches that, from the beginning of time to the beginning of Jesus' own ministry to your life today, human beings are involved in a spiritual battle. Your faith does not exclude you from this spiritual battle—rather it puts you right in the midst of it.

What does the Bible say about spiritual warfare?

1 PETER 5:8 | *Stay alert! Watch out for your great enemy, the devil. He prowls around like a roaring lion, looking for someone to devour.*

You must be alert at all times for the sneak attacks of the devil.

JAMES 4:7 | *Resist the devil, and he will flee from you.*

When you resist the devil in the name and power of Jesus, he will flee from you. At the name of Jesus, Satan has no power.

MATTHEW 4:4 | *Jesus told [the devil], "No! The Scriptures say, . . ."*

When Jesus was under attack by the tempter, he relied on the Word of God to resist the lies of his adversary.

Promise from God EPHESIANS 6:11 | *Put on all of God's armor so that you will be able to stand firm against all strategies of the devil.*

STEWARDSHIP

What does it mean to be a good steward?

LEVITICUS 25:23 | *[The Lord said,] "The land belongs to me. You are only foreigners and tenant farmers working for me."*

MATTHEW 24:45-47 | *A faithful, sensible servant is one to whom the master can give the responsibility of managing his other household servants and feeding them. If the master returns and finds that the servant has done a good job, there will be a reward. I tell you the truth, the master will put that servant in charge of all he owns.*

ROMANS 14:12 | *Yes, each of us will give a personal account to God.*

Good stewardship of your financial resources means that you carefully think about your money and try to spend and save it wisely. But often we forget that God calls us to be good stewards of all the resources and gifts he has provided for us to use and enjoy. Since he has invested so much in us, as evidenced by his amazing plan of salvation and the gift of eternal life, we should invest our time and talents—all of which he has given us—in his work and in other people until he returns. The goal of stewardship is to make the best possible use of what we have in order to make the greatest possible impact on others so that God's work can move forward as efficiently and effectively as possible.

How does God want me to use the resources available to me?

DEUTERONOMY 16:17 | *All must give as they are able, according to the blessings given to them by the LORD your God.*

PROVERBS 3:9 | *Honor the LORD with your wealth and with the best part of everything you produce.*

As you are able, give your best to God's servants and God's work, even to the point of personal sacrifice.

LUKE 3:11 | *John replied, "If you have two shirts, give one to the poor. If you have food, share it with those who are hungry."*

ROMANS 12:13 | *When God's people are in need, be ready to help them. Always be eager to practice hospitality.*

Use your resources to help others who are in need. Share what you have with a generous heart as often as you can.

1 CORINTHIANS 6:19-20 | *Don't you realize that your body is the temple of the Holy Spirit, who lives in you and was given to*

you by God? You do not belong to yourself, for God bought you with a high price. So you must honor God with your body.

Take care of your body so you will be strong and healthy to serve God and others.

LUKE 12:48 | *When someone has been given much, much will be required in return; and when someone has been entrusted with much, even more will be required.*

You are ultimately accountable to God for how you use your gifts and opportunities. God entrusts certain resources to people and then expects them to maximize their effectiveness through wise and godly stewardship. While the most talented people may seem to be the most blessed, they are also required to be the most responsible.

Promise from God MATTHEW 25:21 | *Well done, my good and faithful servant. You have been faithful in handling this small amount, so now I will give you many more responsibilities.*

STRENGTHS/WEAKNESSES

How do I discover my strengths and weaknesses?

DANIEL 1:4 | *"Select only strong, healthy, and good-looking young men," [the king] said. "Make sure they are well versed in every branch of learning, are gifted with knowledge and good judgment, and are suited to serve in the royal palace. Train these young men in the language and literature of Babylon."*

Often your strengths are more evident to others than to yourself. Seek the advice of others to help you determine your strengths and weaknesses. Ask the Holy Spirit to reveal how he has especially gifted you and to show you your strengths and how you can use them to serve God.

How can I take full advantage of my strengths and minimize my weaknesses?

EXODUS 36:1 | *The LORD has gifted Bezalel, Oholiab, and the other skilled craftsmen with wisdom and ability to perform any task involved in building the sanctuary. Let them construct and furnish the Tabernacle, just as the LORD has commanded.*

1 CORINTHIANS 12:7 | *A spiritual gift is given to each of us so we can help each other.*

Use your strengths and skills to build and serve the church.

ECCLESIASTES 4:12 | *A person standing alone can be attacked and defeated, but two can stand back-to-back and conquer. Three are even better, for a triple-braided cord is not easily broken.*

Join with others to help you minimize your weaknesses and maximize your strengths.

ECCLESIASTES 10:10 | *Using a dull ax requires great strength, so sharpen the blade. That's the value of wisdom; it helps you succeed.*

God can give you wisdom to know how to more fully develop your strengths.

1 CORINTHIANS 4:7 | *What gives you the right to make such a judgment? What do you have that God hasn't given you? And if everything you have is from God, why boast as though it were not a gift?*

Remember to give God the full credit for whatever strengths you have.

JEREMIAH 20:11 | *The LORD stands beside me like a great warrior. Before him my persecutors will stumble. They cannot defeat me.*

2 CORINTHIANS 12:9 | *[The Lord] said, "My grace is all you need. My power works best in weakness." So now I am glad to boast about my weaknesses, so that the power of Christ can work through me.*

God will stand beside you and give you strength when you are weak. Dedicate your weaknesses as well as your strengths to serving him.

Promise from God EPHESIANS 3:20 | *All glory to God, who is able, through his mighty power at work within us, to accomplish infinitely more than we might ask or think.*

STRESS

What causes stress?

JAMES 1:2-4 | *When troubles come your way, consider it an opportunity for great joy. For you know that when your faith is tested, your endurance has a chance to grow. So let it grow, for when your endurance is fully developed, you will be perfect and complete, needing nothing.*

Adversity and the normal problems of life cause stress.

GENESIS 3:6, 23 | *[Eve] took some of the fruit and ate it. Then she gave some to her husband, who was with her, and he ate it, too. . . . So the LORD God banished them from the Garden of Eden.*

2 SAMUEL 11:4; 12:13-14 | *David sent messengers to get her; and when she came to the palace, he slept with her. . . . Nathan replied, ". . . The LORD has forgiven you, and you won't die for this sin. Nevertheless, . . . your child will die."*

Often stress is the result of your own actions. Sin brings painful consequences.

How can I deal with stress?

PSALM 55:22 | *Give your burdens to the LORD, and he will take care of you. He will not permit the godly to slip and fall.*

PSALM 86:7 | *I will call to you whenever I'm in trouble, and you will answer me.*

JOHN 14:1 | *[Jesus said,] "Don't let your hearts be troubled. Trust in God, and trust also in me."*

Stress comes when you fail to trust God for help. The first step in dealing with stress is to bring your burdens to the Lord. Only he can give you true peace of heart and mind. God's availability and promises are effective stress reducers.

MATTHEW 11:28-29 | *Jesus said, "Come to me, all of you who are weary and carry heavy burdens, and I will give you rest. Take my yoke upon you. Let me teach you, because I am humble and gentle at heart, and you will find rest for your souls."*

When you allow Jesus to carry your burdens and teach you from his humble and gentle spirit, your stress will melt away and you will instead experience peacefulness in your soul. Jesus' humility and gentleness counteract the pride and irritability that fuel so much of the conflict and stress in life.

Promise from God JOHN 16:33 | *[Jesus said,] "I have told you all this so that you may have peace in me. Here on earth you will have many trials and sorrows. But take heart, because I have overcome the world."*

STUBBORNNESS

What makes people stubborn?

DEUTERONOMY 1:43 | *This is what I told you, but you would not listen. Instead, you again rebelled against the LORD's command and arrogantly went into the hill country to fight.*

Stubbornness is almost always rooted in pride, when people think they know best.

JUDGES 2:19 | *When the judge died, the people returned to their corrupt ways, behaving worse than those who had lived before them. They went after other gods, serving and worshiping them. And they refused to give up their evil practices and stubborn ways.*

Stubbornness can come from resisting authority. Those who enjoy a lifestyle of sin and refuse to give up sinful habits are stubbornly resisting God's authority.

1 SAMUEL 8:19 | *The people refused to listen to Samuel's warning. "Even so, we still want a king," they said.*

Stubbornness can come from a fiercely independent spirit that causes people to be overly self-reliant. The Hebrews wanted an earthly king to rule them, not God.

How can I keep from being stubborn?

2 CHRONICLES 30:8 | *Do not be stubborn, as they were, but submit yourselves to the LORD.*

Submit to God's leading in your life by obeying him and his Word. Don't insist on doing things your way—doing things God's way brings greater joy and fulfillment to your life.

1 CHRONICLES 16:11 | *Search for the LORD and for his strength; continually seek him.*

Seek God's wisdom and guidance before you form opinions and make decisions.

HEBREWS 3:13 | *You must warn each other every day, while it is still "today," so that none of you will be deceived by sin and hardened against God.*

Fellowship with other believers, including exhorting and warning one another, can keep you accountable for your actions and preserve you from developing a hard heart.

EXODUS 8:19 | *"This is the finger of God!" the magicians exclaimed to Pharaoh. But Pharaoh's heart remained hard. He wouldn't listen to them, just as the LORD had predicted.*

When you see God's work around you, give God the credit and the praise.

Promise from God JEREMIAH 3:17 | *All nations will come there to honor the LORD. They will no longer stubbornly follow their own evil desires.*

SUCCESS

Is it okay to try to achieve material success in this life?

PROVERBS 12:24 | *Work hard and become a leader; be lazy and become a slave.*

PROVERBS 22:29 | *Do you see any truly competent workers? They will serve kings rather than working for ordinary people.*

Many godly character traits, such as hard work, integrity, commitment, serving others, and planning, may certainly (but not always) bring material success.

GENESIS 39:2-3 | *The LORD was with Joseph, so he succeeded in everything he did as he served in the home of his Egyptian master. Potiphar noticed this and realized that the LORD was with Joseph, giving him success in everything he did.*

JOB 42:12, 16-17 | *The LORD blessed Job in the second half of his life even more than in the beginning. . . . Job lived 140 years after that, living to see four generations of his children and grandchildren. Then he died, an old man who had lived a long, full life.*

Throughout the Scriptures, there are frequent references to material blessings God has given his people. He sometimes allows his people to have and enjoy material blessings, but he urges them never to forget the One who gave them. It is always a bad investment to sacrifice spiritual riches for worldly wealth.

What is success in God's eyes?

MATTHEW 22:37 | *Jesus replied, "'You must love the LORD your God with all your heart, all your soul, and all your mind.'"*

JOHN 17:3 | *This is the way to have eternal life—to know you, the only true God, and Jesus Christ, the one you sent to earth.*

Success is knowing God and living in a way that pleases him. It is loving him with everything you have—your heart, soul, and mind. The more you know him, the more you will love him, because he is worthy of your worship.

2 CORINTHIANS 5:9-10 | *Whether we are here in this body or away from this body, our goal is to please him. For we must all stand before Christ to be judged. We will each receive whatever we deserve for the good or evil we have done in this earthly body.*

Success is pleasing God. Form your agenda from God's agenda. Ultimately your goals should be rooted in what you can achieve with integrity, in ways consistent with loving God and others.

PSALM 119:28 | *Encourage me by your word.*

PSALM 119:54 | *Your decrees have been the theme of my songs wherever I have lived.*

Knowing and following God's Word brings success, for God's Word reveals his will for your life, and that is the most successful path you can take. God's Word teaches you truth; whatever is true can be counted on, and whatever can be counted on will give you a strong foundation on which to live your life. It will equip you with the skills and understanding you need to live life to the fullest.

JOSHUA 1:8-9 | *Study this Book of Instruction continually. Meditate on it day and night so you will be sure to obey everything written in it. Only then will you prosper and succeed in all you do. This is my command—be strong and courageous! Do not be afraid or discouraged. For the LORD your God is with you wherever you go.*

EPHESIANS 6:10-11, 13 | *Be strong in the Lord and in his mighty power. Put on all of God's armor so that you will be able to stand firm against all strategies of the devil. . . . Then after the battle you will still be standing firm.*

You will be successful in your life as a Christian when you commit yourself to vigorous spiritual training and preparation. Begin by reading God's Word consistently and inviting God to be part of your everyday life. When you consistently obey God's Word, you will experience victory over your fears; over Satan's tactics to derail your relationship with God; and, ultimately, over sin and death. Then you will experience incredible joy.

MATTHEW 20:26 | *Among you it will be different. Whoever wants to be a leader among you must be your servant.*

Serving and helping others brings success, for in serving others you find true joy.

JOHN 15:8, 16 | *[Jesus said,] "When you produce much fruit, you are my true disciples. This brings great glory to my Father. . . . You didn't choose me. I chose you. I appointed you to go and produce lasting fruit, so that the Father will give you whatever you ask for, using my name."*

Success is being productive by doing things that matter to God. The Bible calls this bearing fruit. This kind of fruit comes as a result of your relationship with Jesus and your commitment to living by the principles of success that he taught.

Promise from God PSALM 84:11 | *The LORD God is our sun and our shield. He gives us grace and glory. The LORD will withhold no good thing from those who do what is right.*

SUFFERING

Why am I suffering? Doesn't God care about me?

GENESIS 37:28 | *When the Ishmaelites, who were Midianite traders, came by, Joseph's brothers pulled him out of the cistern and sold him to them for twenty pieces of silver.*

JEREMIAH 32:18 | *You show unfailing love to thousands, but you also bring the consequences of one generation's sin upon the next.*

Sometimes you may be suffering because of the sins of others. There are natural consequences of sin that spill over to those around the sinner.

JOHN 9:2-3 | *"Rabbi," his disciples asked him, "why was this man born blind? Was it because of his own sins or his parents' sins?" "It was not because of his sins or his parents' sins," Jesus answered.*

Sometimes the suffering that comes to you is not your fault or anyone else's—it just happens. We live in a fallen world where sin is often allowed to run its course, affecting believers and nonbelievers alike (see Matthew 5:45). God doesn't want to see you suffer, but the great message of the Bible is that he promises to bring renewal, healing, and spiritual maturity through it so that you can be stronger and better equipped to help others and to live with purpose and meaning. Your reaction to the suffering is what matters, not whose fault it is.

GENESIS 3:6, 23 | *The woman was convinced. She saw that the tree was beautiful and its fruit looked delicious, and she wanted the wisdom it would give her. So she took some of the fruit and ate it. Then she gave some to her husband, who was with her, and he ate it, too. . . . So the LORD God banished them from the Garden of Eden, and he sent Adam out to cultivate the ground from which he had been made.*

LEVITICUS 26:43 | *At last the people will pay for their sins, for they have continually rejected my regulations and despised my decrees.*

PROVERBS 3:11-12 | *My child, don't reject the LORD's discipline, and don't be upset when he corrects you. For the LORD corrects those he loves, just as a father corrects a child in whom he delights.*

Sometimes God sends suffering as punishment for your sin. He disciplines you because he loves you—he wants to correct you and restore you to him. Thank God for this kind of suffering, because his action to get your attention could save you from even greater consequences.

DEUTERONOMY 8:2 | *Remember how the LORD your God led you through the wilderness for these forty years, humbling you and testing you to prove your character, and to find out whether or not you would obey his commands.*

Sometimes God tests you with suffering to encourage you to obey him.

1 PETER 4:14 | *Be happy when you are insulted for being a Christian, for then the glorious Spirit of God rests upon you.*

Sometimes suffering comes because you take a stand for Jesus.

JAMES 1:3 | *When your faith is tested, your endurance has a chance to grow.*

Sometimes you are allowed to suffer because it will help you grow and mature.

2 TIMOTHY 3:12 | *Everyone who wants to live a godly life in Christ Jesus will suffer persecution.*

The world hates Christ, so when you identify with him, you can expect the world that inflicted suffering on him will also inflict suffering on you.

How do I stay close to God in times of suffering?

PSALM 22:24 | *He has not ignored or belittled the suffering of the needy. He has not turned his back on them, but has listened to their cries for help.*

Recognize that God has not abandoned you in your suffering.

PSALM 126:5-6 | *Those who plant in tears will harvest with shouts of joy. They weep as they go to plant their seed, but they sing as they return with the harvest.*

Recognize that suffering is not forever. In the dark hours of the night of suffering, it is hard to think of a morning of joy and gladness. But tears of suffering water seeds of joy.

LAMENTATIONS 3:32-33 | *Though [God] brings grief, he also shows compassion because of the greatness of his unfailing love. For he does not enjoy hurting people or causing them sorrow.*

Recognize that our loving God does not want to see you suffer when hard times come your way. But you can trust that his compassionate love and care will see you through your times of discipline and pain.

MATTHEW 17:12 | *In the same way they will also make the Son of Man suffer.*

LUKE 24:26 | *Wasn't it clearly predicted that the Messiah would have to suffer all these things before entering his glory?*

JOHN 3:16 | *God loved the world so much that he gave his one and only Son, so that everyone who believes in him will not perish but have eternal life.*

HEBREWS 2:18 | *Since he himself has gone through suffering and testing, he is able to help us when we are being tested.*

Recognize that Jesus himself suffered for you. He not only suffered the physical agonies of the cross but also bore the unfathomable weight of the sins of the world.

ROMANS 8:17-18 | *Since we are his children, we are his heirs. In fact, together with Christ we are heirs of God's glory. But if we are to share his glory, we must also share his suffering. Yet what we suffer now is nothing compared to the glory he will reveal to us later.*

Recognize that all suffering will end and that there is a glorious future awaiting all those who believe in Jesus.

Can any good come from suffering?

JOB 5:17-18 | *Consider the joy of those corrected by God! Do not despise the discipline of the Almighty when you sin. For though he wounds, he also bandages. He strikes, but his hands also heal.*

Sometimes you are suffering because you are dealing with the consequences of your sin. In that case, you can learn from your mistakes and avoid repeating them in the future. At other times, your suffering is the result of hardships outside your control. During those times, you have the opportunity to learn and grow, so you should take advantage of each opportunity. It will help you deal better with suffering in the future, and it will teach you to recognize and avoid certain troubles down the road.

Promise from God   2 CORINTHIANS 1:3-4 | *All praise to God, the Father of our Lord Jesus Christ. God is our merciful Father and the source of all comfort. He comforts us in all our troubles so that we can comfort others. When they are troubled, we will be able to give them the same comfort God has given us.*

TEMPTATION

Does temptation ever come from God?

MARK 7:15 | *It's not what goes into your body that defiles you; you are defiled by what comes from your heart.*

JAMES 1:13 | *God is never tempted to do wrong, and he never tempts anyone else.*

Temptation never comes from God; it comes from Satan, who plants it in your heart.

JAMES 1:2 | *When troubles come your way, consider it an opportunity for great joy.*

Although God does not send temptation, he brings good from it by helping you grow stronger through it.

What makes temptation so enticing?

GENESIS 3:6 | *The woman . . . saw that the tree was beautiful and its fruit looked delicious. . . . So she took some of the fruit and ate it.*

Satan's favorite strategy is to make that which is sinful appear desirable and good.

1 KINGS 11:1, 3 | *King Solomon loved many foreign women. . . .
And in fact, they did turn his heart away from the LORD.*

Often temptation begins with seemingly harmless
pleasure, but soon it gets out of control and progresses
to full-blown sin.

How can I resist temptation?

GENESIS 39:12 | *[Potiphar's wife] came and grabbed him by
his cloak, demanding, "Come on, sleep with me!" Joseph tore
himself away, but he left his cloak in her hand as he ran from
the house.*

If possible, remove yourself from the tempting situation.
Sometimes you must literally run from it.

PROVERBS 1:10 | *My child, if sinners entice you, turn your back
on them!*

Sometimes the greatest temptations come from those you
think are your friends. If you know you are liable to give
in to pressure from certain people, it is best to avoid their
company.

MATTHEW 6:13 | *Don't let us yield to temptation, but rescue
us from the evil one.*

Make resisting temptation a constant focus of your prayers.

TITUS 2:12 | *We are instructed to turn from godless living and
sinful pleasures.*

Christian growth brings an increased awareness and sensi-
tivity to temptation in your life.

Promise from God   1 CORINTHIANS 10:13 | *The temptations in your life are no different from what others experience. And God is faithful. He will not allow the temptation to be more than you can stand. When you are tempted, he will show you a way out so that you can endure.*

THOUGHTS

How can I please God with my thoughts?

JOSHUA 1:8 | *Study this Book of Instruction continually. Meditate on it day and night so you will be sure to obey everything written in it. Only then will you prosper and succeed in all you do.*

PSALM 119:11 | *I have hidden your word in my heart, that I might not sin against you.*

1 TIMOTHY 4:13, 15 | *Focus on reading the Scriptures to the church, encouraging the believers, and teaching them. . . . Give your complete attention to these matters.*

God is pleased when you think about his Word. Study and think about God's Word continually until it fills your mind.

1 CHRONICLES 28:9 | *[David said,] "Solomon, my son, learn to know the God of your ancestors intimately. Worship and serve him with your whole heart and a willing mind. For the LORD sees every heart and knows every plan and thought. If you seek him, you will find him. But if you forsake him, he will reject you forever."*

MATTHEW 22:37 | *You must love the LORD your God with all your heart, all your soul, and all your mind.*

It pleases God when your thoughts are full of love for him.

MATTHEW 5:28 | *Anyone who even looks at a woman with lust has already committed adultery with her in his heart.*

MARK 7:20-23 | *Then [Jesus] added, "It is what comes from inside that defiles you. For from within, out of a person's heart, come evil thoughts, sexual immorality, theft, murder, adultery, greed, wickedness, deceit, lustful desires, envy, slander, pride, and foolishness. All these vile things come from within; they are what defile you."*

Don't allow your mind to dwell on sinful thoughts. Bad thoughts are bound to pop into your mind, but it's when you allow them to stay that you get in trouble. When bad thoughts come to mind, don't entertain them—immediately turn to God in prayer.

PSALM 19:14 | *May the words of my mouth and the meditation of my heart be pleasing to you, O LORD, my rock and my redeemer.*

PSALM 26:2 | *Put me on trial, LORD, and cross-examine me. Test my motives and my heart.*

PSALM 139:23 | *Search me, O God, and know my heart; test me and know my anxious thoughts.*

Ask God to help you have pure thoughts by inviting him to examine your mind and convict you whenever you are thinking wrong things.

PHILIPPIANS 4:8 | *Fix your thoughts on what is true, and honorable, and right, and pure, and lovely, and admirable. Think about things that are excellent and worthy of praise.*

Make a conscious effort to practice thinking good thoughts, just as you might practice some other skill. These thoughts might be about the good in your life that you can be thankful for, the good in others that you appreciate, the good that you might do for others, or the goodness of God in providing you with earthly blessings and promising you eternal life.

COLOSSIANS 3:2-3 | *Think about the things of heaven, not the things of earth. For you died to this life, and your real life is hidden with Christ in God.*

Think more about heaven, because someday it will be your eternal home.

ROMANS 12:2 | *Don't copy the behavior and customs of this world, but let God transform you into a new person by changing the way you think. Then you will learn to know God's will for you, which is good and pleasing and perfect.*

Be prepared to let God radically change not only what you think about but the way you think.

Promise from God 1 CHRONICLES 29:17 | *I know, my God, that you examine our hearts and rejoice when you find integrity there.*

TITHING

Why did God require tithes from his people in the Old Testament?

LEVITICUS 27:30 | *One-tenth of the produce of the land, whether grain from the fields or fruit from the trees, belongs to the LORD and must be set apart to him as holy.*

NUMBERS 18:20, 23-24 | *The LORD said to Aaron, "You priests will receive no allotment of land or share of property among the people of Israel. I am your share and your allotment. . . . The Levites will receive no allotment of land among the Israelites, because I have given them the Israelites' tithes, which have been presented as sacred offerings to the LORD. This will be the Levites' share."*

The tithes were necessary to support the priesthood—the ordained spiritual leaders who were responsible for Israel's worship and the spiritual lives of the people.

DEUTERONOMY 14:22-23 | *You must set aside a tithe of your crops— one-tenth of all the crops you harvest each year. . . . Doing this will teach you always to fear the LORD your God.*

Giving one-tenth of their income to God taught the Israelites to make him a priority in their lives, to acknowledge their dependence on him, and to sacrifice for the well-being of others.

Am I required to tithe to God today?

1 TIMOTHY 5:17-18 | *Elders who do their work well should be respected and paid well, especially those who work hard at both preaching and teaching. For the Scripture says, "You must not muzzle an ox to keep it from eating as it treads out the grain." And in another place, "Those who work deserve their pay!"*

The need to financially support the spiritual leaders of the church has not changed from the Old to the New Testament or to today.

PHILIPPIANS 4:18-19 | *I am generously supplied with the gifts you sent me with Epaphroditus. . . . And this same God who takes care of me will supply all your needs from his glorious riches, which have been given to us in Christ Jesus.*

While you may wonder how much value there is in the little bit that you can offer God, remember that the purpose of tithing is to give you the privilege of participating in God's work. Giving to God can help you learn to meet the needs of others, just as God gives to meet your needs.

PROVERBS 3:9 | *Honor the LORD with your wealth and with the best part of everything you produce.*

Giving to God first from your paycheck honors him by demonstrating that he has first priority in your life.

MATTHEW 5:42 | *Give to those who ask, and don't turn away from those who want to borrow.*

ROMANS 12:8 | *If your gift . . . is giving, give generously.*

When you give, give generously as you share with others.

2 CORINTHIANS 9:7 | *You must each decide in your heart how much to give. And don't give reluctantly or in response to pressure. "For God loves a person who gives cheerfully."*

Old Testament law made it clear that God wanted his people to tithe—to give him the first tenth of their income to demonstrate obedience and trust that he would provide for them. When Jesus came, he made it clear that he loves a cheerful giver. This means that he loves a generous heart. Whatever the amount, you should honor the Lord with your wealth so that his work on earth can boldly continue. God promises to bless you lavishly if you give lavishly.

MATTHEW 23:23 | *You should tithe, yes, but do not neglect the more important things.*

Jesus affirmed the need to give tithes to God.

PROVERBS 21:13 | *Those who shut their ears to the cries of the poor will be ignored in their own time of need.*

1 CORINTHIANS 16:1-2 | *Now regarding your question about the money being collected for God's people in Jerusalem. . . . On the first day of each week, you should each put aside a portion of the money you have earned.*

God wants you to give in order to take care of those who are less fortunate.

Promises from God MALACHI 3:10 | *"Bring all the tithes into the storehouse so there will be enough food in my Temple. If you do," says the LORD of Heaven's Armies, "I will open the windows of heaven for you. I will pour out a blessing so great you won't have enough room to take it in! Try it! Put me to the test!"*

LUKE 6:38 | *Give, and you will receive. Your gift will return to you in full—pressed down, shaken together to make room for more, running over, and poured into your lap. The amount you give will determine the amount you get back.*

VALUES

How do I assess my current values?

PROVERBS 30:8 | *First, help me never to tell a lie.*

ROMANS 1:29 | *Their lives became full of every kind of wickedness, sin, greed, hate, envy, murder, quarreling, deception, malicious behavior, and gossip.*

EPHESIANS 5:4 | *Obscene stories, foolish talk, and coarse jokes—these are not for you. Instead, let there be thankfulness to God.*

How do you view those things that the Bible calls sin, such as gossip, flattery, profanity, lying, and cheating? If you don't see these as sins, you must face up to the fact that your values differ from God's.

MATTHEW 15:19 | *From the heart come evil thoughts, murder, adultery, all sexual immorality, theft, lying, and slander.*

The heart is the source of moral or immoral behavior. If your actions don't regularly match up with what God says is right, then you need a change of heart before you can change your behavior.

How can I cultivate godly values?

GENESIS 39:8-9 | *Joseph refused. "Look," he told her, "my master trusts me with everything in his entire household. . . . He has held back nothing from me except you, because you are his wife. How could I do such a wicked thing? It would be a great sin against God."*

Refuse the kind of lifestyle choices the Bible says are worthless or dangerous to your long-term well-being. To obey God's Word is to align your values with God's.

PSALM 15:1-2 | *Who may worship in your sanctuary, LORD? . . . Those who lead blameless lives and do what is right, speaking the truth from sincere hearts.*

MICAH 6:8 | *O people, the LORD has told you what is good, and this is what he requires of you: to do what is right, to love mercy, and to walk humbly with your God.*

MATTHEW 7:12 | *Do to others whatever you would like them to do to you. This is the essence of all that is taught in the law and the prophets.*

GALATIANS 5:22-23 | *The Holy Spirit produces this kind of fruit in our lives: love, joy, peace, patience, kindness, goodness, faithfulness, gentleness, and self-control. There is no law against these things!*

Godly living simply means valuing what God values. To have godly values, you need God living in you. He promises that when you ask him, he will send his Holy Spirit to live in you, helping you to value and to live out what is truly important.

How important is it to live a consistently moral life?

EXODUS 23:24 | *You must not worship the gods of these nations or serve them in any way or imitate their evil practices.*

PSALM 24:3-4 | *Who may climb the mountain of the LORD? Who may stand in his holy place? Only those whose hands and hearts are pure, who do not worship idols and never tell lies.*

PROVERBS 28:2 | *When there is moral rot within a nation, its government topples easily.*

Strong moral values demonstrate that your commitment to be a follower of God is genuine. They are also essential to the well-being of any society.

Promise from God ROMANS 5:3-5 | *We can rejoice, too, when we run into problems and trials, for we know that they help us develop endurance. And endurance develops strength of character, and character strengthens our confident hope of salvation. And this hope will not lead to disappointment. For we know how dearly God loves us, because he has given us the Holy Spirit to fill our hearts with his love.*

VULNERABILITY

In what areas of my life should I allow myself to be vulnerable?

PSALM 139:23-24 | *Search me, O God, and know my heart; test me and know my anxious thoughts. Point out anything in me that offends you, and lead me along the path of everlasting life.*

HEBREWS 4:12-13 | *The word of God is alive and powerful. It is sharper than the sharpest two-edged sword, cutting between soul and spirit, between joint and marrow. It exposes our innermost thoughts and desires. Nothing in all creation is hidden from God. Everything is naked and exposed before his eyes, and he is the one to whom we are accountable.*

It is essential to fully open your heart and life to God and let him do his work in you to help you become all he created you to be. If you hold back from God and don't allow him to help, you will never reach your God-given potential.

GENESIS 2:25 | *The man and his wife were both naked, but they felt no shame.*

Next to your relationship with God, you should be most vulnerable with your wife. There should be nothing hidden between the two of you.

2 CORINTHIANS 11:27 | *I have worked hard and long, enduring many sleepless nights. I have been hungry and thirsty and have often gone without food. I have shivered in the cold, without enough clothing to keep me warm.*

Serving God might make you vulnerable at times to difficulty and danger.

MATTHEW 5:11-12 | *[Jesus said,] "God blesses you when people mock you and persecute you and lie about you and say all sorts of evil things against you because you are my followers. Be happy about it! Be very glad! For a great reward awaits you in heaven. And remember, the ancient prophets were persecuted in the same way."*

HEBREWS 10:33 | *Sometimes you were exposed to public ridicule and were beaten, and sometimes you helped others who were suffering the same things.*

Allow yourself to be vulnerable enough to endure humiliation and ridicule for believing in Jesus.

How can I help those who are vulnerable?

GENESIS 9:22-23 | *Ham, the father of Canaan, saw that his father was naked and went outside and told his brothers. Then Shem and Japheth took a robe, held it over their shoulders, and backed into the tent to cover their father. As they did this, they looked the other way so they would not see him naked.*

PSALM 82:4 | *Rescue the poor and helpless; deliver them from the grasp of evil people.*

PROVERBS 23:10 | *Don't cheat your neighbor by moving the ancient boundary markers; don't take the land of defenseless orphans.*

PROVERBS 31:9 | *Speak up for the poor and helpless, and see that they get justice.*

When people are vulnerable, they are easily taken advantage of. Do what you can to "cover" those who are vulnerable and to protect them from being exploited.

JOB 6:14 | *One should be kind to a fainting friend.*

ISAIAH 58:7 | *Share your food with the hungry, and give shelter to the homeless. Give clothes to those who need them, and do not hide from relatives who need your help.*

Help those who are vulnerable in order to restore them to a stronger position. You do this by treating them with mercy, compassion, and kindness and by providing whatever resources you can.

Promise from God PSALM 12:5 | *The LORD replies, "I have seen violence done to the helpless, and I have heard the groans of the poor. Now I will rise up to rescue them, as they have longed for me to do."*

WISDOM

What are the benefits of having wisdom?

ECCLESIASTES 10:10 | *Using a dull ax requires great strength, so sharpen the blade. That's the value of wisdom; it helps you succeed.*

Wisdom will help you to succeed in whatever you do.

EPHESIANS 5:15 | *Be careful how you live. Don't live like fools, but like those who are wise.*

Wisdom helps you know how to live.

1 KINGS 3:9 | *[Solomon said,] "Give me an understanding heart so that I can govern your people well and know the difference between right and wrong."*

The more responsibility you have, the more you need God's wisdom in order to do what is right.

PROVERBS 3:21-26 | *My child, don't lose sight of common sense and discernment. Hang on to them, for they will refresh your soul. They are like jewels on a necklace. They keep you safe on your way, and your feet will not stumble. You can go to bed without fear; you will lie down and sleep soundly. You need not be afraid of sudden disaster or the destruction that comes upon the wicked, for the LORD is your security. He will keep your foot from being caught in a trap.*

Wisdom will help preserve you from trouble and disaster.

PROVERBS 9:11-12 | *Wisdom will multiply your days and add years to your life. If you become wise, you will be the one to benefit. If you scorn wisdom, you will be the one to suffer.*

Wisdom will give you a richer, fuller life.

How can I obtain wisdom?

JOB 28:28 | *The fear of the Lord is true wisdom; to forsake evil is real understanding.*

PROVERBS 9:10 | *Fear of the LORD is the foundation of wisdom. Knowledge of the Holy One results in good judgment.*

Giving God first place in your life is a prerequisite for obtaining God's wisdom. Asking God for wisdom is a hollow request if you are not willing to let him rule in your heart. Wisdom comes from fearing God.

1 JOHN 2:27 | *You have received the Holy Spirit, and he lives within you, so you don't need anyone to teach you what is true. For the Spirit teaches you everything you need to know, and what he teaches is true—it is not a lie. So just as he has taught you, remain in fellowship with Christ.*

Wisdom comes from the Holy Spirit, who lives in you when you believe in Jesus Christ.

PROVERBS 1:5-6 | *Let the wise listen to these proverbs and become even wiser. Let those with understanding receive guidance by exploring the meaning in these proverbs and parables, the words of the wise and their riddles.*

Obedience to God's Word—his commands, laws, and teachings—will make you wise.

JAMES 1:5 | *If you need wisdom, ask our generous God, and he will give it to you. He will not rebuke you for asking.*

If you need wisdom, ask God; he's promised to give it to you.

PSALM 86:11 | *Teach me your ways, O LORD, that I may live according to your truth! Grant me purity of heart, so that I may honor you.*

COLOSSIANS 3:16 | *Let the message about Christ, in all its richness, fill your lives. Teach and counsel each other with all the wisdom he gives.*

Listening to Christ's teachings and obeying his words will give you wisdom.

PROVERBS 8:12, 17 | *I, Wisdom, live together with good judgment. I know where to discover knowledge and discernment. . . . I love all who love me. Those who search will surely find me.*

You find wisdom when you pursue it wholeheartedly.

Promise from God PROVERBS 24:5 | *The wise are mightier than the strong, and those with knowledge grow stronger and stronger.*

WITNESSING

How important is witnessing?

PSALM 107:2 | *Has the LORD redeemed you? Then speak out! Tell others he has redeemed you from your enemies.*

MARK 16:15 | *[Jesus] told them, "Go into all the world and preach the Good News to everyone."*

God wants you to tell others about what he has done.

MARK 1:17 | *Jesus called out to them, "Come, follow me, and I will show you how to fish for people!"*

ACTS 10:42 | *He ordered us to preach everywhere and to testify that Jesus is the one appointed by God to be the judge of all— the living and the dead.*

Telling others the story of Jesus is an essential part of being his follower. Simply tell others why you love him; God promises to soften the hearts of many who listen.

2 KINGS 7:9 | *This is not right. This is a day of good news, and we aren't sharing it with anyone! . . . Come on, let's go back and tell the people at the palace.*

It is not right to keep the Good News to yourself. Your witness may be the only way some people will ever hear the Good News.

ROMANS 10:14-15 | *How can they call on him to save them unless they believe in him? And how can they believe in him if they have never heard about him? And how can they hear about him unless someone tells them? And how will anyone go and tell them without being sent?*

The only way people can be saved is by hearing and believing the message of the Good News that we have.

EZEKIEL 3:18 | *If I warn the wicked, saying, "You are under the penalty of death," but you fail to deliver the warning, they will die in their sins. And I will hold you responsible for their deaths.*

You have a responsibility to tell others about Jesus whenever the opportunity arises.

JUDE 1:23 | *Rescue others by snatching them from the flames of judgment. Show mercy to still others, but do so with great caution, hating the sins that contaminate their lives.*

Tell others the message of salvation to spare them from judgment.

What should my witnessing include?

EXODUS 18:9 | *Jethro was delighted when he heard about all the good things the LORD had done for Israel as he rescued them from the hand of the Egyptians.*

JOHN 9:25 | *"I don't know whether he is a sinner," the man replied. "But I know this: I was blind, and now I can see!"*

Your witness should include telling others how God has rescued you and freed you from the burden of sin.

PSALM 28:6 | *Praise the LORD! For he has heard my cry for mercy.*

Tell others about the prayers God has answered.

PSALM 30:3 | *You brought me up from the grave, O LORD. You kept me from falling into the pit of death.*

Explain how God has saved you from spiritual death.

ACTS 4:33 | *The apostles testified powerfully to the resurrection of the Lord Jesus, and God's great blessing was upon them all.*

Be sure to tell others about the resurrection of Jesus, because this is the basis for your hope of eternal life.

ACTS 10:42 | *He ordered us to preach everywhere and to testify that Jesus is the one appointed by God to be the judge of all— the living and the dead.*

Warn people about the ultimate judgment of God that awaits.

1 PETER 3:15 | *If someone asks about your Christian hope, always be ready to explain it.*

Be ready to explain why you have hope.

1 JOHN 1:2 | *Now we testify and proclaim to you that he is the one who is eternal life.*

Tell others the good news that eternal life is found in Christ.

1 CORINTHIANS 2:2 | *I decided that while I was with you I would forget everything except Jesus Christ, the one who was crucified.*

Tell how Jesus died on the cross to take away your sins.

LUKE 24:47 | *It was also written that this message would be proclaimed in the authority of his name to all the nations, beginning in Jerusalem: "There is forgiveness of sins for all who repent."*

Explain the message of repentance, forgiveness, and reconciliation with God.

ROMANS 10:9 | *If you confess with your mouth that Jesus is Lord and believe in your heart that God raised him from the dead, you will be saved.*

Make clear the need to confess Christ as Lord and believe in his resurrection.

1 THESSALONIANS 1:5 | *When we brought you the Good News, it was not only with words but also with power, for the Holy Spirit gave you full assurance that what we said was true. And you know of our concern for you from the way we lived when we were with you.*

How you live is an important element of your witness for Jesus. Make sure your actions match your words.

Promise from God DANIEL 12:3 | *Those who are wise will shine as bright as the sky, and those who lead many to righteousness will shine like the stars forever.*

WIVES

How does God want a man to treat his wife?

PROVERBS 18:22 | *The man who finds a wife finds a treasure, and he receives favor from the LORD.*

God wants you to treat your wife as the treasure she really is.

GENESIS 2:23 | *"At last!" the man exclaimed. "This one is bone from my bone, and flesh from my flesh! She will be called 'woman,' because she was taken from 'man.'"*

You should treat your wife with an attitude of deep appreciation.

1 CORINTHIANS 7:3, 5 | *The husband should fulfill his wife's sexual needs, and the wife should fulfill her husband's needs. . . . Do not deprive each other of sexual relations.*

Give her tender love and sexual intimacy.

1 CORINTHIANS 7:32-33 | *An unmarried man can spend his time doing the Lord's work and thinking how to please him. But a married man has to think about his earthly responsibilities and how to please his wife.*

Sometimes you must forgo your own plans or ministries in order to take care of your wife and please her.

EPHESIANS 5:23 | *A husband is the head of his wife as Christ is the head of the church. He is the Savior of his body, the church.*

A husband must exercise responsibility and leadership, which involves sacrificial service to his wife.

EPHESIANS 5:25, 28-29, 33 | *For husbands, this means love your wives, just as Christ loved the church. . . . Husbands ought to love their wives as they love their own bodies. . . . No one hates his own body but feeds and cares for it. . . . Each man must love his wife as he loves himself.*

COLOSSIANS 3:19 | *Husbands, love your wives and never treat them harshly.*

Love your wife with sacrificial love, and treat her with gentleness and kindness.

1 PETER 3:7 | *You husbands must give honor to your wives. Treat your wife with understanding as you live together. She may be weaker than you are, but she is your equal partner in God's gift of new life.*

Honor your wife and be understanding.

How does God want a woman to treat her husband?

JUDGES 13:22-23 | *He said to his wife, "We will certainly die, for we have seen God!" But his wife said, "If the LORD were going to kill us, he . . . wouldn't have appeared to us and told us this wonderful thing and done these miracles."*

MATTHEW 27:19 | *As Pilate was sitting on the judgment seat, his wife sent him this message: "Leave that innocent man* alone. I suffered through a terrible nightmare about him last night."

Sometimes a woman needs to give loving counsel and advice to her husband. A husband should expect that at times his wife will have wisdom and spiritual insight beyond his.

JOB 2:9-10 | *[Job's] wife said to him, "Are you still trying to maintain your integrity? Curse God and die." But Job replied, ". . . Should we accept only good things from the hand of God and never anything bad?"*

A wife should respect her husband's wisdom and spiritual insight in situations where she lacks them.

HEBREWS 13:4 | *Give honor to marriage, and remain faithful to one another in marriage. God will surely judge people who are immoral and those who commit adultery.*

You should expect that your wife will be faithful to you in marriage, as you are faithful to her.

2 CHRONICLES 21:6 | *Jehoram followed the example of the kings of Israel and was as wicked as King Ahab, for he had married one of Ahab's daughters. So Jehoram did what was evil in the LORD's sight.*

A husband should expect that his wife will influence his decisions, either for good or for evil.

Promise from God PROVERBS 18:22 | *The man who finds a wife finds a treasure, and he receives favor from the LORD.*

WORDS

Do my words really matter?

DEUTERONOMY 23:23 | *Once you have voluntarily made a vow, be careful to fulfill your promise to the LORD your God.*

JOSHUA 9:19-20 | *The leaders replied, "Since we have sworn an oath in the presence of the LORD, the God of Israel, we cannot touch them. This is what we must do. We must let them live, for divine anger would come upon us if we broke our oath."*

When you say you will do something, people should be able to trust that you will do it. Trust is vital for a Christian's witness.

PSALM 15:1-3 | *Who may worship in your sanctuary, LORD? Who may enter your presence on your holy hill? Those who lead blameless lives and do what is right, speaking the truth from sincere hearts. Those who refuse to gossip or harm their neighbors or speak evil of their friends.*

Only those who speak truth and kindness can enter God's presence and worship. Your words matter to God because they reveal the motives of your heart.

JAMES 1:26 | *If you claim to be religious but don't control your tongue, you are fooling yourself, and your religion is worthless.*

Your words show what kind of person you really are. You are living a double standard if you speak one way in church and another way at home, at work, or in the community.

PROVERBS 11:11 | *Upright citizens are good for a city and make it prosper, but the talk of the wicked tears it apart.*

PROVERBS 15:1 | *A gentle answer deflects anger, but harsh words make tempers flare.*

Words of blessing and words of anger are equally powerful. You can greatly help or hinder those around you by what you say.

PROVERBS 17:9 | *Love prospers when a fault is forgiven, but dwelling on it separates close friends.*

Your words make a difference in your relationships.

MATTHEW 12:36-37 | *[Jesus said,] "You must give an account on judgment day for every idle word you speak. The words you say will either acquit you or condemn you."*

The words you speak during your life can condemn or justify you on Judgment Day.

What kinds of words should I speak?

GENESIS 50:21 | *[Joseph] reassured them by speaking kindly to them.*

Speak kind words to others.

PSALM 50:23 | *Giving thanks is a sacrifice that truly honors me.*

ROMANS 15:6 | *All of you can join together with one voice, giving praise and glory to God, the Father of our Lord Jesus Christ.*

Speak words of thanks and praise to God.

EPHESIANS 4:29 | *Let everything you say be good and helpful, so that your words will be an encouragement to those who hear them.*

Use words that encourage others and build them up.

PROVERBS 15:4 | *Gentle words are a tree of life; a deceitful tongue crushes the spirit.*

PROVERBS 25:15 | *Patience can persuade a prince, and soft speech can break bones.*

Speak to others with gentleness and patience.

1 PETER 3:9 | *Don't repay evil for evil. Don't retaliate with insults when people insult you. Instead, pay them back with a blessing. That is what God has called you to do, and he will bless you for it.*

Use your words to bless even those who hurt you.

ZECHARIAH 8:16 | *This is what you must do: Tell the truth to each other. Render verdicts in your courts that are just and that lead to peace.*

Speak truthfully.

Promise from God PROVERBS 10:20 | *The words of the godly are like sterling silver.*

WORK

Does God care what kind and quality of work I do?

ECCLESIASTES 12:14 | *God will judge us for everything we do, including every secret thing, whether good or bad.*

God cares about what you do and how well you do it.

1 KINGS 11:28 | *Jeroboam was a very capable young man, and when Solomon saw how industrious he was, he put him in*

charge of the labor force from the tribes of Ephraim and Manasseh, the descendants of Joseph.

ECCLESIASTES 9:10 | *Whatever you do, do well.*

You should be industrious and do your best in your work.

PROVERBS 13:11 | *Wealth from get-rich-quick schemes quickly disappears; wealth from hard work grows over time.*

Honest, hard work is much better than schemes to get rich quickly.

PROVERBS 26:13-16 | *The lazy person claims, "There's a lion on the road! Yes, I'm sure there's a lion out there!" As a door swings back and forth on its hinges, so the lazy person turns over in bed. Lazy people take food in their hand but don't even lift it to their mouth. Lazy people consider themselves smarter than seven wise counselors.*

2 THESSALONIANS 3:11-12 | *We hear that some of you are living idle lives, refusing to work and meddling in other people's business. We command such people and urge them in the name of the Lord Jesus Christ to settle down and work to earn their own living.*

You should earn your own living, instead of finding excuses not to work.

How can I balance work and family?

PSALM 39:6 | *We are merely moving shadows, and all our busy rushing ends in nothing.*

ECCLESIASTES 5:3 | *Too much activity gives you restless dreams; too many words make you a fool.*

Even though you are called to work hard, you must make sure your work doesn't preoccupy you to the extent that you endanger your health, your relationships, or your time with God.

ACTS 16:16 | *One day as we were going down to the place of prayer, we met a demon-possessed slave girl. She was a fortune-teller who earned a lot of money for her masters.*

You must make sure that your profession doesn't compromise your values.

EXODUS 16:23 | *Tomorrow will be a day of complete rest, a holy Sabbath day set apart for the LORD.*

MARK 6:31 | *Jesus said, "Let's go off by ourselves to a quiet place and rest awhile."*

There is a time to stop your work in order to rest, to celebrate, and to worship God.

Promise from God ECCLESIASTES 5:19 | *To enjoy your work and accept your lot in life—this is indeed a gift from God.*

WORRY

When does worry become sin?

MATTHEW 13:22 | *The seed that fell among the thorns represents those who hear God's word, but all too quickly the message is crowded out by the worries of this life and the lure of wealth, so no fruit is produced.*

COLOSSIANS 3:2 | *Think about the things of heaven, not the things of earth.*

Worry is like thorny weeds—left uncontrolled, it crowds out what is good. Worry over the concerns of life becomes sin when it prevents the Word of God from taking root in your life. Worry is a misuse of your God-given imagination!

How can I worry less?

PSALM 55:4-5 | *My heart pounds in my chest. The terror of death assaults me. Fear and trembling overwhelm me, and I can't stop shaking.*

Worry and fear are normal responses to threatening situations, but often you imagine far worse scenarios than what actually happens. Recognize that most worries never come to pass.

EXODUS 14:13 | *Moses told the people, "Don't be afraid. Just stand still and watch the LORD rescue you today."*

Combat worry and anxiety by remembering and trusting what God, in his Word, has promised to do for you.

PHILIPPIANS 4:6 | *Don't worry about anything; instead, pray about everything.*

When you place your cares in Jesus' hands, you don't have to worry.

PSALM 62:6 | *He alone is my rock and my salvation, my fortress where I will not be shaken.*

When you remember that God's love and care for you are as solid as a rock, you can keep your worries in perspective. He has everything under control.

MATTHEW 6:27 | *Can all your worries add a single moment to your life?*

Instead of adding more time or improving the quality of your life, worry robs you of your health and takes away your joy.

Promise from God   1 PETER 5:7 | *Give all your worries and cares to God, for he cares about you.*

WORSHIP

How is worship integral to my relationship with God?

1 CHRONICLES 16:29 | *Give to the LORD the glory he deserves! Bring your offering and come into his presence. Worship the LORD in all his holy splendor.*

PSALM 145:3 | *Great is the LORD! He is most worthy of praise! No one can measure his greatness.*

Worship is recognizing who God is and who you are in relation to him. It is remembering his many acts of love toward you and then praising him in return.

EXODUS 29:43 | *I will meet the people of Israel there, in the place made holy by my glorious presence.*

DEUTERONOMY 31:11 | *You must read this Book of Instruction to all the people of Israel when they assemble before the LORD your God at the place he chooses.*

MICAH 4:2 | *Come, let us go up to the mountain of the LORD, to the house of Jacob's God. There he will teach us his ways, and we will walk in his paths.*

Something very powerful and unique happens when God's people sing, praise, hear his Word, and worship him together. There is a sense of community and fellowship that can only happen in corporate worship.

PSALM 5:7 | *Because of your unfailing love, I can enter your house; I will worship at your Temple with deepest awe.*

ISAIAH 6:3 | *They were calling out to each other, "Holy, holy, holy is the LORD of Heaven's Armies! The whole earth is filled with his glory!"*

Worship is a fitting response to God's holiness, power, and grace.

REVELATION 4:9-11 | *Whenever the living beings give glory and honor and thanks to the one sitting on the throne (the one who lives forever and ever), the twenty-four elders fall down and worship the one sitting on the throne (the one who lives forever and ever). And they lay their crowns before the throne and say, "You are worthy, O Lord our God, to receive glory and honor and power. For you created all things, and they exist because you created what you pleased."*

Worshiping God is a foretaste of heaven.

What does worshiping God involve? How should I worship God?

GENESIS 35:2-3 | *Jacob told everyone in his household, "Get rid of all your pagan idols, purify yourselves, and put on clean clothing. We are now going to Bethel, where I will build an altar to the God who answered my prayers when I was in distress. He has been with me wherever I have gone."*

DEUTERONOMY 11:16 | *Don't let your heart be deceived so that you turn away from the LORD and serve and worship other gods.*

Worship only God, because he alone is worthy of your utmost devotion.

EXODUS 3:5 | *"Do not come any closer," the LORD warned. "Take off your sandals, for you are standing on holy ground."*

When you approach God's presence in worship, recognize that wherever you are, you are standing on holy ground.

PSALM 35:18 | *I will thank you in front of the great assembly. I will praise you before all the people.*

Your worship should include praise and thanks to God for what he has done.

PSALM 95:6 | *Come, let us worship and bow down. Let us kneel before the LORD our maker.*

Kneeling and bowing are appropriate postures for worship.

1 CHRONICLES 13:8 | *David and all Israel were celebrating before God with all their might, singing songs and playing all kinds of musical instruments—lyres, harps, tambourines, cymbals, and trumpets.*

Worship can also take the form of a joyous celebration, with musical instruments and singing.

HEBREWS 12:28 | *Since we are receiving a Kingdom that is unshakable, let us be thankful and please God by worshiping him with holy fear and awe.*

Respect and awe for what is holy should accompany thanksgiving as appropriate attitudes in worship.

AMOS 5:21 | *[The Lord says,] "I hate all your show and pretense—the hypocrisy of your religious festivals and solemn assemblies."*

Public worship is useless if it is done without sincerity and the desire to live wholeheartedly for God.

Promise from God PHILIPPIANS 2:9-11 | *God elevated [Christ Jesus] to the place of highest honor and gave him the name above all other names, that at the name of Jesus every knee should bow, in heaven and on earth and under the earth, and every tongue confess that Jesus Christ is Lord, to the glory of God the Father.*